Pg. 37 Opposite elements
Frustration

Elements & Crosses
as the Basis of the Horoscope

pg 73

The element says something about :
  person's view of the world
  attitude of consciousness
  way nature/experiences/judges everything met

The crosses provide information about processes
of adapting to events & circumstances as
well as the processes of assimilation and
adaptation

73-94 Summary of Interpretation !

Elements & Crosses
as the Basis of the Horoscope

by

Drs. Karen Hamaker-Zondag

Translated from the Dutch by Transcript

The Jungian Symbolism & Astrology Series

Volume 1

SAMUEL WEISER, INC.
York Beach, Maine

Translated from the Dutch by transcript
Original title: *Elementen en Kruizen*
als Basis van de Horoscoop:
Deel 1, De Astrologische Duiding
First published in 1979 by
W. N. Schors, Amsterdam

English translation published in 1984 by
Samuel Weiser, Inc.
Box 612
York Beach, Maine 03910

ISBN 0-87728-523-3
Library of Congress Catalog Card Number: 82-50535

Typeset by Positive Type

Printed by Mitchell-Shear, Inc.
in the United States of America

Table of Contents

LIST OF CHARTS

INTRODUCTION

Following the appearance of my book *Astro-Psychology*, many people asked if I would write a handbook elaborating its ideas and showing how they could be carried out in practice. I have gladly fulfilled that request. In this first volume, *Elements and Crosses as the Basis of the Horoscope,* I am introducing a concept that has proven to be an invaluable basis for horoscope interpretation. In the next three volumes of this series, I will continue to expand on this basis.

Many astrological reference books supply the reader with a definition of the planets in the signs, the aspects, etc., and are otherwise quite helpful; yet for all sorts of practical reasons they tend to omit any guidelines for combining the unique personal information symbolized by the horoscope itself. Therefore, it often remains unclear why a certain aspect has a strong effect in one horoscope while in another that same aspect may seem to do very little. Before analyzing a horoscope using information from reference books, we need to build a framework which forms a basis for all the factors that are to be interpreted.

In my opinion, astrological literature has paid too little attention to the construction of such a framework. Because of this lack, we run into a number of contradictions, and it is difficult to ascertain what conditions actually will appear in the person's life. After much investigation and many comparisons with analytical

Sign	Symbol	Day Ruler Night Ruler		Element	Cross
Aries	♈	Mars Pluto	♂ ♇	Fire	Cardinal
Taurus	♉	Venus —	♀	Earth	Fixed
Gemini	♊	Mercury —	☿	Air	Mutable
Cancer	♋	Moon —	☽	Water	Cardinal
Leo	♌	Sun —	☉	Fire	Fixed
Virgo	♍	Mercury —	☿	Earth	Mutable
Libra	♎	Venus —	♀	Air	Cardinal
Scorpio	♏	Pluto Mars	♇ ♂	Water	Fixed
Sagittarius	♐	Jupiter Neptune	♃ ♆	Fire	Mutable
Capricorn	♑	Saturn Uranus	♄ ♅	Earth	Cardinal
Aquarius	♒	Uranus Saturn	♅ ♄	Air	Fixed
Pisces	♓	Neptune Jupiter	♆ ♃	Water	Mutable

psychology, I have seen that the symbolism, background, and function of both the elements and the crosses—separately and in relationship to one another—serve as a basis for interpreting the horoscope. If astrologers are to use this system, the basis must be completely practical in its application. This book is, in fact, a continuation and more profound study of my theoretical *Astro-Psychology*. I have tried to explain things so that one can begin working without having read my first book. Naturally, I assume the reader has some acquaintance with the meanings of the signs and the houses, thereby needless repetition can be avoided. To clarify the symbols and signs used in the charts for my American readers, see the table provided.

I owe many thanks to Maggie Schors, Fred Molenberg, and my husband Hans for their many sensible comments about the original manuscript; the text was written with enthusiasm, and thanks to them it became much more readable.

Amsterdam, June, 1983

To my colleagues

in the Astrological Foundation *ARCTURUS*

CHAPTER ONE

THE BASIS OF THE HOROSCOPE

1. TOTALITY OF THE PSYCHE

A concept central to psychology is that of "psychic totality," which includes both the conscious and unconscious sides of our psyche. Both sides are complementary in proportion; they are opposite and yet complete each other in all respects. Man identifies, however, only with the conscious part of his psyche, the part that says "I," seldom able to realize the important role his personal and collective unconscious plays. Every moment of the day the unconscious forces itself upon him in countless ways, whether convenient or not. Sometimes it manifests as a "Freudian slip" which makes it clear that other factors are alive in him, or perhaps it expresses as an inexplicable but especially helpful brainstorm or suggestion that comes from within.

Immanuel Kant considered the question of whether man had an unconscious, although he used other words for it. In *Anthropology* he wrote:

> ...the area of sensations and sense impressions in man (and also in animals), of which we are not aware (although undoubtedly we can affirm its existence), is unfathomable; this is the area of "obscure" images. With its opposite, the area of "lucid" images, it shares but very few points of contact open to the conscious mind. That so few areas of the great map of our mind, as it were, are

> illumined should awaken wonder in us as to our true
> being. A higher power would only need to cry, "Let there
> be light!", and even without the slightest action on
> anyone's part, *half* a world would be shown to him....
> since the area of "obscure" images is the largest in man.[1]

It is obvious that Kant meant the same with his "area of obscure or
dark images" as an analytical psychologist does when he speaks of
man's unconscious. That unconscious can never become completely
conscious; only certain portions of it can become clear to man
during the course of his life. Kant also talked about the fact that our
consciousness can reach no more than half of our psyche—half a
world.

We can discover much about the structure of the unconscious
through the study of people's behavior, associations, and emotions.
Through countless forms of unconscious expression (dreams,
fantasies, slips of the tongue, etc.) we can gradually form an idea of
its structure and operation. We will still be unable to grasp it with
our conscious minds, as the unconscious functions completely
independently and autonomously. Goethe once said:

> ...a human being should not stay too rigidly fixed in a
> condition of unconsciousness or ordinary consciousness;
> he must return to the refuge of his unconscious for there
> lie his roots.[2]

Goethe hereby indicated that there is a difference between the
conscious and the unconscious psyche. The unconscious must be
considered in any psychological approach to astrology if we want to
arrive at a balanced and total view. Consciousness allows man to
experience his world, to comprehend and understand, and—in our
Western culture—to adapt to outer reality, to which this side of the
psyche is geared. The unconscious, on the other hand, is geared to
adapting to inner reality.

---

[1]Kant, Immanuel, Anthropologie, par. 5. Citation from: Psychologische Club Zürich:
Die Kulturelle Bedeutung der Komplexen Psychologie. Festschrift zum 60. Geburt-
stag von C.G. Jung, Berlin, 1935. Teil I: Toni Wolff: Einführung in die Grundlagen
der Komplexen Psychologie, p. 52.

[2]*Ibid*, p. 54. Goethe made this statement to Riemer on August 5, 1810.

A concept such as *consciousness* can give rise to much confusion if not clearly defined. Nowadays, it begins more and more to mean insight or the broadening of insight, and many people think it is very positive to "live consciously" or "to be conscious." In psychology, however, *consciousness* has a distinct meaning which shows little agreement with what most people ordinarily understand by the term. In the latter case perhaps we can better speak of awareness and reserve the term consciousness for psychology. By consciousness Carl Jung understands the following:

> . . .the relation of psychic contents to the ego, in so far as this relation is perceived as such by the ego. Relations to the ego that are not perceived as such are unconscious.[3]

The psyche consists of two complementary spheres that show opposite qualities: consciousness and the unconscious. The ego can share in both spheres; all experiences from both the inner and the outer world must go via the ego in order to be perceived. Consciousness is thereby further described by Jung as ". . .the function or activity which maintains the relation of psychic contents to the ego."[4] The ego he describes as ". . .a complex of ideas which constitutes the centre of my field of consciousness and appears to possess a high degree of continuity and identity."[5]

Consciousness has the function of relaying information to the ego, which possesses a particular constancy regarding its readiness to consider certain information important and applicable to itself and other information not so important. The ego may not want to see some things consciousness passes on to it. These incidents or ideas are then repressed and disappear from consciousness into the unconscious. Repressed contents can begin to lead their own life there, penetrating the field of consciousness now and then where they deliver painful 'dents' to the ego or may even contribute to correcting an ego that has become too one-sided.

---

[3] Jung, C.G., *Psychological Types*, Collected Works, Vol 6, Routledge & Kegan Paul, London, 1977, pp. 421-422.

[4] Jacobi, J., *The Psychology of C.G. Jung*, Routledge & Kegan Paul, London, 1973, p. 16.

[5] *Ibid*, p. 16.

Jolande Jacobi already noticed at an early stage the possible confusions around the concept of consciousness and expressed it as follows:

> ...In common parlance 'consciousness' is often used interchangeably with 'thinking', although this is inadmissible, for there is a consciousness of feeling, will, fear, as well as other life phenomena. Nor should the idea of 'life' be equated with 'consciousness', which unfortunately frequently happens. A person who is asleep is alive and yet not conscious. There are different degrees of consciousness. Perceiving something is an act of consciousness, in which, however, the perceived has not as yet been assimilated; it remains as it were passive compared with a conscious, discriminating, understanding, assimilating attitude.[6]

In his textbook *Bewusstsein*, C.A. Meier has elucidated a clear example of the confusion surrounding the term consciousness. I repeat it here in its entirety so as not to remove it from context:

> ...Here we are faced with a paradox. Awareness would be the product of a synthesis between consciousness and the unconscious. This is reminiscent of an expression which has become current in analytical psychology jargon and which often leads to misunderstandings: people used to be fond of saying that somebody was 'very unconscious', meaning with this that such a person solely acts according to conscious motives. But from an analytical viewpoint this means that he does not include his unconscious backgrounds in the discussion so that it is generally correct to say that this person clearly acts according to conscious motives and therefore should be very aware. The object of analytical psychology is, however, to make man also aware of his unconscious motivations and to postpone any decision making until he achieves this clarity in himself. Not until then would such an individual, according to our terminology, really

[6]*Ibid*, p. 16.

deserve the predicate 'aware', in other words not until the moment when he has resolved the conflict made conscious in this way and has taken a decision...[7]

2. CONSCIOUSNESS AND THE FOUR ELEMENTS

Although the contents of the human consciousness are infinite, we can order them so they reveal a clear structure and a typical form. That is, one can distinguish between general behavior and certain forms of behavior that are peculiar to a certain group of individuals.[8] These behavior patterns can be reduced to the way one consciously adapts to reality, the specific manner of approaching and comprehending the world. We can distinguish four different elementary processes of consciousness, which show a remarkable similarity with the four elements of astrological tradition, namely:

Sensation: perceiving as such and seeing what the object is like, for instance—hard, sharp, warm, etc. This corresponds to the element earth.

Thinking: asking *what* the perceived object actually is and how it can be incorporated into the existing frame of reference. This corresponds to the element air.

Feeling: experiencing what the perceived object calls forth in the way of desire or aversion, on the grounds of which it is accepted or rejected. For instance: is it pleasurable or not, is it nice or not? This corresponds to the element water.

Intuition: unconscious knowing or "inferring" where the perceived object comes from or how it will evolve further. Often the object is not consciously perceived, but is instead a sort of "sensing" of the background. Jung called this a form of indirect perception. This function corresponds to the element fire.

---

[7]Meier, C.A., *Bewusstsein*. Erkenntnistheorie und Bewusstsein. Bewusstwerdung bei C.G. Jung, Wather Verlag, Olten, 1975, p. 16.

[8]Wolff, T., *Studien zu C.G. Jungs Psychologie*, Rhein Verlag, Zürich, 1959, p. 81.

In order to show how different functions approach the same information, Jung once gave the following example:[9]

1. *Sensation:* I see that something is red, that it has a certain sheen and sparkle, a certain form and smell.

2. *Thinking:* I recognize this object as a glass filled with red wine.

3. *Feeling:* I judge the whole; I find it extremely pleasing. For a teetotaller it would be a highly repellent object, however.

4. *Intuition:* I suppose that it is a Pommard 1937 and that it could be a Christmas present from my host's friend X.

Concerning intuition, Jung often emphasized that the accuracy of the intuitive type is less than fifty percent in most cases. Whether the intuition is right or not, the essential point is that the intuitive type approaches the phenomena around him in a certain *manner*. This type will continually look behind things without knowing it or without consciously seeing the object or phenomenon as such, while the sensation type will automatically see what the object or phenomenon looks like and how it presents itself. The four functions of consciousness don't say whether the contents are good or bad; primarily, they express a certain way of approaching things with consciousness.

Together all four functions form a complete view of a situation or a complete consideration of an object. Astrologically, this means the four elements combine to form a whole, a totality that theoretically would make it possible to observe, appraise, see through and experience *all* facets of a given object or phenomenon.

Since each individual's consciousness can only have one superior function, one main orientation, on the basis of the four elements we can distinguish four general types. They always remain general types because so many factors come into play, depending upon each individual horoscope. One can speak of types to a greater or lesser degree. Some people may have a conscious orientation or

---

[9]Meier, C.A., *Bewusstsein*. Lehrbuch der Komplexen Psychologie C.G. Jungs. Band III. Wather Verlag, Olten, 1975, p. 133-134.

superior element made up of a combination of two elements or psychological functions, and one of them will always predominate (see Section 4 in this chapter). These general types are of great importance, as they illustrate how a person relates to the world around him, how he experiences, views, and judges it. The following material introduces the main characteristics of the four elements or the four types of functions: fire, earth, air and water.[10]

THE FIRE OR INTUITIVE TYPE

The fire signs, Aries, Leo and Sagittarius, live mainly in a world hidden behind the material existence. Concepts such as *the future, possibility, discovery* and *dynamic* play a large role in the world of the fire type. Life and all of its material and non-material manifestations are seen from the inside out by the fire type, as he intuitively feels how everything is or could be. For him the world is a story full of fantastic possibilities in which he plays an important role.

The person with a strong fire influence is self-centered and therefore makes an egoistic and insensitive impression, a trait of which he is seldom aware. He lives according to his own morals and is faithful to his own ideas as far as they allow him perspectives and possibilities. Routine work may be unbearable, as it kills his spontaneity and constricts his irrepressible activities. Through his rather open, expectant, and sometimes naive attitude, he is receptive to experience, seeking its meaning and possibility. Through this attitude of consciousness, he can acquire deep insights into hidden connections. Concrete facts and objects play no role for him. In daily life, he can be almost helpless in practical affairs because he is always seeing behind things and not the things themselves.

[10]For a more comprehensive and detailed description of the four types the following books are recommended: von Franz, M.-L., & J. Hillman, *Lectures on Jung's Typology*, Spring Verlag, Zürich, 1971; Greene, Liz, *Relating: An astrological guide to living with others on a small planet*, Samuel Weiser, Inc., York Beach, Me., 1977, Chapter 3; Hamaker-Zondag, K.M., *Astro-Psychology*, Aquarian Press, Wellingborough, 1980. Chapter 4; Jung, C.G., *Psychological Types*, Routledge & Kegan Paul, London, 1971. Chapter 10; Whitmont, E.C., *The Symbolic Quest: Basic Concepts of Analytical Psychology*, Princeton University Press, Princeton, 1969, Chapter 8.

THE EARTH OR SENSATION TYPE

The signs Taurus, Virgo and Capricorn react in an exactly opposite manner than the fire signs. If looking behind appearances was central for fire, here perceiving concrete facts themselves forms the central idea. Everything possible is felt out and tested for its concrete value with the senses. Reality and efficiency are concepts that belong to this type. Things that can't be perceived with the senses simply don't exist for the earth type. Earth will have precious little understanding of the fantasy world of the fire signs, a fantasy world that is just as real for the fire type as the earth itself.

The consciousness of the earth type is geared to concrete experience, a reason why so much value is placed on outward beauty: *beautiful* is something that can be perceived concretely and judged accordingly. The fire sign's search for possibility is something that would only give rise to anxiety in an earth sign: the danger for earth is that he might lose all he's built up in the way of material security for something he can't or doesn't want to imagine. Therefore, out of a need for security, the earth type builds for a future that offers a solid, practical basis; he will aim for it with purpose, energy and a tenacious ability to persevere. Because the earth type seeks a foundation in concrete facts and actualities, he runs the danger of missing the essential relationships between things, which his experience can only coordinate with difficulty, if at all. On the other hand, dedication to the concrete and material gives this type an outstanding feeling for form and proportion.

THE AIR OR THINKING TYPE

What earth neglects—namely the connection between facts—is precisely the strong side of the air signs Gemini, Libra, and Aquarius. In this element, the emphasis is on abstract thought, theory and ideas. Consciousness is directed at the most logical, objective approach and assimilation of the things observed or experienced. The air signs gladly discuss their findings with others, being known for their ability to communicate. Through the logical process of thinking and exchange, the air type is often flexible in speech and action, though this flexibility can become so exaggerated that there may be little stability.

Air examines the behavior of those around him as well as his own for logic; thus the air type runs the danger of being too rational in his motives and can appear to be cool and unfeeling. His attempts to force life into a mold of rigid formulas and motives without taking the value of feelings into account can be self-defeating. An emotional approach to things poses difficulties for him, as his feelings can't be rationalized, nor can they be captured in words. His emotional life is his weakest area.

The consciousness of the air type is aimed at combining objects and ideas as logically as possible; this combination is the frame of reference from which he judges how life should be. On the whole, he has no sense of the realistic value of his thoughts and theories; they form reality for him, *his* reality, just as a fantasy world is reality for a fire type. This is why an air type doesn't need to be practical; practicality is a typical earth quality.

THE WATER OR FEELING TYPE

Where air is least at home, we find the water signs Cancer, Scorpio and Pisces developing their greatest capacities. These signs predominantly perceive and evaluate the world in an emotional way. The logical connection between things, so important to the air signs, doesn't play a direct role. For water types the feeling evoked by a person, object or situation is important. Everything is judged on this basis.

For consciousness, feeling is an almost inexplicable process, even when feeling is the specific means through which one views the world. It gives a certain form of "after the event" consciousness; in other words, the water sign is able to identify (unintentionally) with someone else and become that person to such a degree that he only later learns to establish his own identity on the basis of all that he is *not*.

A deep, sensitive, and emotional involvement in events is characteristic for water signs, even though they don't necessarily show it. Sensitivity can make them so vulnerable that they tend to hide behind an unemotional mask, one reason why a water type doesn't always come across as a warm, sensitive, and empathetic type. The feeling process can take hold of this type to such an extent that the outside world only serves as impulse, bringing the process into motion or sustaining it, so that a warm reaction doesn't need to follow. The element of water can then be "cold" to the touch as well.

Because water consciousness orients itself through the feeling function, it needs constant stimulation from outside. That need often makes water signs demanding, yearning, absorbing, and clinging. Through emotional contact with the outside world, they can literally feel things that can't be explained. They come so close to the core of a situation they sometimes hit the nail on the head. Bringing their conclusions into words is a difficult business for them for that reason.

WEIGHING THE IMPORTANCE OF EACH ELEMENT

Every element has its essential and special way of looking at life experience. None of the elements has more or less value than another and we all have the four. The four elements together form a totality. If we could approach a situation with our thinking, feeling, sensation, and intuitive consciousness, then and only then, could we come to a truly conclusive judgment about that situation. Consciousness, however, is always using one or two functions or elements, with the other elements operating from the unconscious. It is outside the ability of human consciousness to give a perfectly complete and balanced judgment. No matter how objective a person attempts to be, his judgment will always be colored by his own personality. Understanding our own element division can reveal our own *coloration,* the glasses we see through.

Everyone has all the elements in his horoscope: the circle contains the whole zodiac and is always the basis of the horoscope. With each of us, the relationship between the elements is different, in many cases one or two elements are over-emphasized. This is completely in agreement with the experience of psychology which speaks of one superior function, helped perhaps by one or sometimes two important auxiliary functions.

In establishing the division of elements in a horoscope, it is an error to simply sum up the planets found in that element. We would be ignoring the fact that some planets are more important for human consciousness than others. In the division of elements we should not forget that we have connected the elements with a certain attitude of consciousness. Automatically the more important role is played by the personal planets (the Sun, Moon, Mercury, Venus and Mars). Once we have found the one or two most important elements for consciousness, we know that the remaining elements are connected with the unconscious. In the examples on the following pages, we will go into this more thoroughly.

The most personal and individualized points in the horoscope are the Sun, Moon, Mercury and the Ascendant. The sign on the Midheaven and the ruler of the Ascendant are important, though subordinate to the first group, turning the scale only in case of doubt. Venus and Mars can be called purely personal, though in all cases they are less important than the Sun, Moon, Mercury and the Ascendant. Jupiter and Saturn take an in-between position.

The planets beyond Saturn (Uranus, Neptune and Pluto) can clearly be called impersonal. They are located in the same sign for long periods of history and form more a characteristic of that period of time than direct personal traits. They can give a certain color to one's character if they are important in a particular horoscope—for instance, if they are connected to the personal planets. Their content and meaning are impersonal, and for the most part connected with the unconscious part of the human psyche. Their actions are unverifiable, in great part beyond control, and sometimes sudden (Uranus); in short, human will and consciousness have little grasp of their contents.

When we find a horoscope containing an element comprised of three impersonal planets—for instance, Saturn, Uranus, and Neptune (as was the case in 1942-43 when they were all in air)—and another element containing two personal planets—for instance, the Sun and Moon—that second element will be by far the most important for that person's consciousness, coloring his vision of events much more than the element containing the impersonal planets. The element with the impersonal planet will play a role dependent upon its relation to the element in which the Sun and Moon are found.

In the horoscope, the ego is reflected by the Sun. Generally speaking, the ego identifies with a certain psychological function (or astrological element), so the Sun's element is certainly of great importance. That element doesn't necessarily indicate the dominant conscious function, as the definite answer must come from the rest of the horoscope. However, it has been my experience time and again that the Sun plays a special role in any conclusions about the elements.

3. ESTABLISHING THE ELEMENT DIVISIONS

A fixed rule in astrology is that the planets in the *signs* reflect the *potential* of the person, while the planets in the *houses* reflect the *circumstances*. Experience gained through one's circumstances influences character over the course of time. Often this occurs unconsciously: if someone burns his fingers enough times on a heater, he will finally learn not to touch it impulsively, even if he is reckless by nature. Experience, in this case painful, teaches that something in one's attitude or character must be altered to avoid being hurt. The astrological houses offer a range of experience during a person's lifetime, teaching one how to act in an adequate yet individual way in various areas of life, which doesn't need to follow a set standard. The horoscope shows what actually is *in a*

Element	Sign Number	Sign Name	House
FIRE	1 5 9	Aries Leo Sagittarius	1 5 9
EARTH	2 6 10	Taurus Virgo Capricorn	2 6 10
AIR	3 7 11	Gemini Libra Aquarius	3 7 11
WATER	4 8 12	Cancer Scorpio Pisces	4 8 12

Figure 1.1. The elements and the houses.

Elements	Signs	Houses	Total
FIRE	♃ ☋	☋ ☿	4
EARTH	☿ ☉ ♂ ♄ Mc.	☉ ♂ ♄ ☋	9
AIR	♀ ☋	♀	3
WATER	☋ Asc. ☽	☽ ♃ ☋	6

Figure 1.2. The division of the elements as they appear in the signs and the houses in Fred's chart. (See Chart 1.)

person, not the degree to which this is tolerated by the predominant morality of the time.

Since the houses offer so many possibilities of development, they must be included in any diagram of the elements. The houses reflect not only our circumstances and possibilities for experience, but they also form an essential part of the psyche. When a planet is placed in a certain house, traditional astrology holds that the planet's energy is specifically directed to the area of life symbolized by that house. Consequently, something in one's psyche causes that person to be occupied with these specific matters. In this light, we can hardly deny the ancient law, "As above, so below," which also can be worded "As within, so without." What we contain within us is reflected in our circumstances. As the houses are expressed in specific circumstances, they mirror our inner world, teaching us a great deal about ourselves.[11]

Just as we classify the signs of the zodiac under the elements, we can assign the elements to certain houses, as shown in figure 1.1. The order of the fire *houses* corresponds to that of the fire *signs,* as do the earth *houses* to earth *signs,* etc. Experience has shown that planets in the houses, in so far as they relate to the division of the elements, play an increasingly powerful role as one grows older.

To create a mental picture of the element distribution in any chart, we can separate the elements as shown in figure 1.2. In this

[11]For a comprehensive analysis of this: Hamaker-Zondag, KM., *Astro-Psychology,* Aquarian Press, Wellingborough, 1980, pp. 114-138.

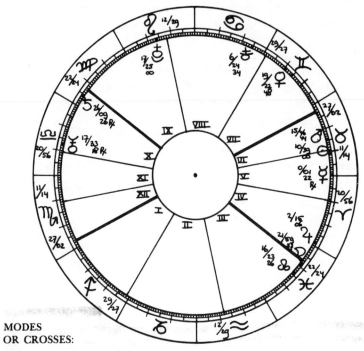

**MODES
OR CROSSES:**

Cardinal:

Fixed:

Mutable:

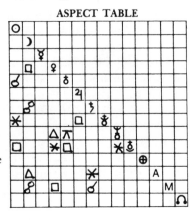

ASPECT TABLE

	Sun	Moon	Mercury	Venus	Mars	Jupiter	Saturn	Uranus	Neptune	Pluto	Part of Fortune	Ascendant	Midheaven	North Node
Sun	☉													
Moon		☽												
Mercury			☿											
Venus		□		♀										
Mars	☌			☍										
Jupiter					♃									
Saturn		☌☌				♄								
Uranus	⚹				□		☿							
Neptune			△	⚺				♀ ☿						
Pluto	□		⚹	□				⚹ ☌						
Part of Fortune									⊕					
Ascendant		△			⚹					A				
Midheaven		☍☌	□		☌						M			
North Node												☊		

ELEMENTS:

Fire:

Earth:

Air:

Water:

illustration we will use the data from Chart 1 on page 14. The four elements are listed so that we can relate them to the zodiacal signs and houses. Next to each element we enter the symbols for the planets posited in the signs of that element. (For example, if Jupiter appears in a fire sign, we put his symbol next to the fire category.) Then we enter the planets posited in *houses* that correspond to the element category. For instance, Mercury may not be in a fire sign (Aries, Leo, Sagittarius) but in this case it is in the 5th house which is a fire sign house in the natural zodiac. We can then determine how many planets affect the various element categories (though it isn't necessary). Entering the planetary symbols on a list such as this provides an immediate view of the distribution of personal and less personal energy.

To determine the element influence by both the planetary sign and house placement, we should always consider the following factors:

a) Although we may determine a total figure on our list, this total can never be used as a quantitative amount in any diagnosis of personality. When you have many planets in one element, if those planets are mostly impersonal, they will not indicate a dominance of that element in consciousness. (The outer planets—Neptune, Uranus and Pluto—cannot be considered to count more strongly than a person's Sun, Moon, and Ascendant, for example.)

b) We work with the concept of ten planets (the Sun and Moon are not planets, but for convenience sake we call them such). Because each planet has two possible categories on our list our total should add up to 20. We can also enter the sign of the Ascendant and the Midheaven (abbreviated as Asc. or A./Mc. or M.) in the "sign" section on our list. We cannot enter them under the "house" section for both positions are always the starting points (or cusps) of the first and tenth houses. Because the Asc. and Mc. are entered only in the sign section, the addition of these two factors brings our total to 22.

Chart 1. This is Fred's chart. He was born May 1, 1951 in Gronigen, Holland at 9:30 pm. The time is from his birth certificate. House system is Placidus. Chart used with permission.

c) Sometimes a planet is located very close to the cusp of the following house, as in the case of the Moon in Chart 1. Such a planet is then considered as belonging to the following house. Although the Moon in our example is located on the cusp of the 4th, we enter it as if it were a part of the fourth house. When looking to determine the energy that forms a personality, any planet that is moving from one house to another will progress to the next house in a very short time after birth. If the cuspal planet is a fast moving one, its influence will probably affect factors of personality described by the next house.

In general, when entering planets in the house section on the list, we can apply the following rules:

a) When a planet is within 4 degrees of the cusp (or starting point) of an *angular* house, it is said to develop its influences in the angular house. The angular houses are the first, fourth, seventh and tenth.

b) If a planet is within 3 degrees of the cusp of any other house, it will be most active in the following house. This rule is applied with a considerably smaller orb (usually about 1 degree) to retrograde planets, such as Neptune in Chart 1. Neptune in our sample chart is within 3 degrees of the cusp of the eleventh house, but because it is retrograde, it remains active in the tenth. Only if it had been located exactly on the cusp would it have been entered in the eleventh house on our list.

Though these rules can be used fairly well in practice, a certain amount of uncertainty is inherent, unless the time of birth is very exact. The slightest deviation in the birth time can alter the house cusps, and therefore alter the sphere of planetary influence as far as the house symbolism is concerned. These rules are valid for determining cuspal influence in the houses only, and should not be used for determining which element a planet is in by sign. For example, if a planet is posited at 29° Leo, its sign cannot be altered. The planet is considered to be in Leo, even though it is very near to the sign of Virgo. If that same planet is at 29° Leo and *also* at the end of the third house, its house position will be entered in the 4th house rather than the third.

4. INTERPRETING THE ELEMENT DIVISION

When we look at *potential* (planets in *signs*) in Fred's horoscope (Chart 1), the strongest category is that of earth. He has Sun, Mercury, and the MC there, followed by the less important Mars. The Sun and Mars repeat themselves in *circumstances* (indicated by planets in *houses*), so the element earth remains strong. The next strongest category is that of water, for it represents the personal nature (Moon and Asc.). The other planet in this element is Uranus, which is not considered a personal one. The Moon is found in a water house as well, so we can also consider this element important.

Mercury is in an earth sign in Chart 1, but it moves to the fire element by house position. However, the fire element holds few personal planets, just as the air element only lays claim to Venus, which repeats itself in air circumstances (houses). It is exceptional when planets repeat the same element by house, and Chart 1 has an above average occurrence of this phenomenon. In conclusion, we can say that the earth element receives the most emphasis on our list. The second most important category is water.

Chart 2 on page 18 (Marilyn Monroe) gives us a completely different picture. As you can see from figure 1.3, without doubt, the element air is most important. Air contains the most personal planets which moreover repeat themselves in air houses. The other three elements are about equal in strength. Water has the most

Elements	Signs	Houses	Total
FIRE	♀ Asc. ♇	♇ ♄	5
EARTH	Mc.	♀	2
AIR	☿ ☉ ☽ ♃	☉ ☿ ♃ ☽	8
WATER	♆ ♄ ♂ ♇	♄ ♂ ♆	7

Figure 1.3. The division of the elements as they appear in the signs and houses in Marilyn Monroe's chart. (See Chart 2.)

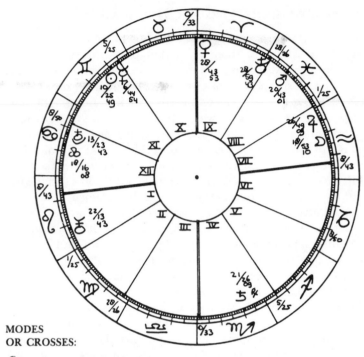

**MODES
OR CROSSES:**

⑦ Cardinal: ♀♂/♅☽♃♀

⑨ Fixed: MC Asc ♄♃♃/♂♀☉

⑥ Mutable: ♆☉♂♅/♄♇

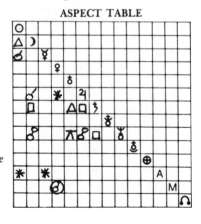

ASPECT TABLE

	Sun	Moon	Mercury	Venus	Mars	Jupiter	Saturn	Uranus	Neptune	Pluto	Part of Fortune	Ascendant	Midheaven	North Node
Sun	☉													
Moon	△	☽												
Mercury	♂		☿											
Venus				♀										
Mars					♂									
Jupiter	☌		✳			♃								
Saturn	□			△□	♄									
Uranus						♅								
Neptune	♂			⊼♂	□		♆							
Pluto							♇							
Part of Fortune								⊕						
Ascendant	✳		✳				A							
Midheaven			⊙					M						
North Node										☊				

ELEMENTS:

Fire: ⑤
♀♂
Asc ♄♅
Earth: ②
MC ♇

Air: ⑧
♅☉☽
♃ ♃☽♀

Water: ⑦
♄☽♆
♅ ♄♂♂

planets, but those are primarily impersonal planets, applying to a whole generation. Venus and the Ascendant are located in fire signs, but Venus is conjunct the Midheaven (and earth circumstance) while there is little further evidence of earth to be found. One element is important for consciousness without a second element ever crystallizing.

In these two examples, it seems fairly simple to name the most important element. There are, however, countless horoscopes where the division is much more difficult. The distribution is so broad that the astrologer can barely make a choice. For instance, someone with the Sun in Aries (fire), the Moon in Taurus (earth), Mercury in Pisces (water), and a Libra Ascendant (air) in potential has the four most important personal indicators in four different elements. The location of these planets in the houses will give a more definite indication. Regardless of which function or element ultimately manifests as most important, *one* important personal content always remains strongly connected with the unconscious of the person in question. Naturally this has specific results for the character structure.

I shall clarify this principle somewhat in a short explanation of the psychology of the four functions of consciousness as far as they are important in astrology. Instead of the expression "function of consciousness" we can use "element" in the strictest astrological sense of the word. We distinguish four different functions of consciousness: thinking, feeling, sensation, and intuition, as we have already described. These four functions can be divided into two pairs—thinking and feeling, which form a judgment about a situation; and sensation and intuition, which perceive a situation. We can call the first pair (thinking and feeling, thus air and water) "judging." Jung called these functions "rational," a word that can be confusing. The judging or rational function is much more occupied with judging an object or situation on the basis of

---

Chart 2. Marilyn Monroe. She was born June 1, 1926 in Los Angeles, California at 9:09 am. Data from Jam Kampherbeek, Holland. House system is Placidus. (Kampherbeek is well known in Holland for the reliability of his data for he collects birth information and doesn't correct charts for his own purposes.)

Inner Tension

∗ o-o {

Thinking — Air

Feeling — Water

} rational/judging function or element

forms judgement about situation

∗ o-o {

Sensation — Earth

Intuition — Fire

} irrational/perceptive function or element

The object itself

Figure 1.4. The elements and functions divide into pairs.

meaning (thinking) or value (feeling) than it is with the actual object or situation in itself.

The other two functions are called perceptive or irrational. (The term irrational as used here is descriptive only and has absolutely no judgmental value!) Sensation (earth) and intuition (fire) restrict themselves much more to the object itself. Sensation perceives how something appears—its form; intuition inwardly perceives where an object came from and how it can develop. In other words, intuition sees the relationship between things in a context independent of time rather than seeing the things themselves. Thereby, it perceives the changing of the form. The pairs look like figure 1.4.

Within the pairs division we can introduce another important division. The functions belonging to a group are always completely opposite each other in the specific and essential view of the world of events implied in these functions. The sensation type is always busy determining the perceptible concreteness of the moment and therefore must ignore all possible past and future changes of form. Otherwise, this type might become distracted by the relationship to other possible, but intangible, objects or situations. If this was done, the individual would no longer be a sensation type. The intuitive type does just the opposite. They both perceive, yet their focus is so contradictory that we can speak of polar opposites. (Therefore, one's awareness of one's own function hardly plays a role.)[12]

[12]A survey of the theory of functions is found in the books listed in footnote 10 by Toni Wolff, C.A. Meier, E.C. Whitmont and M.-L. von Franz.

Two important polarities are found in the division of functions of consciousness. Feeling and thinking (water and air) stand just as diametrically opposite each other as sensation and intuition (earth and fire). In astrological terms, this means that the elements air and water show great tension toward each other because they are psychological opposites, just as are earth and fire. When two important elements belonging to such a dualistic pair become prominent in a certain horoscope, a primary tension will develop. Since the elements are opposites and incompatible, only one function can develop in consciousness while the other necessarily remains associated with the unconscious. There is more inner harmony, or at least less elementary tension, present in horoscopes when two elements appear that are not opposite each other.

In Fred's horoscope, we saw a strong earth-water potential. Earth and water are not in polarity so there isn't a pronounced inner tension on this point. Marilyn Monroe's horoscope, on the other hand, has a strong air potential with water having the next greatest strength. Though the water planets can be called impersonal, they could still cause difficulty since they contrast with the element of consciousness (air).

In conclusion, when we have divided the elements in a horoscope and have determined the most important element, we can soon see if there are deep characterological tensions coming from the major opposing elements or whether these elements are in harmony. The elemental determination of tension is very important for the framework in which we will later analyze the aspects. We can clarify this point by looking at figure 1.5. (See page 22.)

The contrasting elements are always in opposition in a sense, while both elements flanking another element can get along with that element. For instance, water opposes air, but can get along better with earth or fire. See figure 1.6 on page 23. Naturally, when water has to choose between earth and fire, it will choose earth; because like water, it is more introverted, while fire is very exuberant and outgoing. Yet fire will never experience the same tension with water as air does because fire actually understands water better than air (the opposite of water) does. Fire can join the world of water, which is a dream world of fantasy and possibility, without too much logic and theory, without violating its own nature. On the other hand, air, which is opposite water, has little understanding of this attitude, because for air, logic and theory play the main role.

In my practical experience, conflicts in a horoscope arising from non-opposing elements (for instance, a square between Gemini-air and Virgo-earth) are less tense than elements that *are* opposing; for instance, a square between Virgo (earth) and Sagittarius (fire). In evaluating aspects and other important data, the elements play a very important role in the background: the division of elements is one of the basic factors in a horoscope. Inner elementary tension, by the way, should not be given a negative value, because it is just this underlying tension which gives us the impetus to go forward! Determining the amount of tension is the first step in interpreting the division of elements.

The strongest function of consciousness (the strongest element) is what children use to adapt and react to the world. The strongest element must then clearly be present in potential; in other words, with important planets in the signs of that element. In youth, the planets are mainly effective in potential. As we grow older, the houses play a greater role and the totality can begin to work. In both sample horoscopes, the element strongest in potential was also represented by the corresponding houses being strongly occupied, showing influence later in life. (In other words, the air signs might be strongest, but with strong placements in the air houses as well.) When the strength of an element increases in such a way, the attitude developed unconsciously in youth, in agreement with

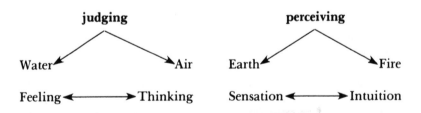

Figure 1.5. The diagram shows the tension that occurs within the framework presented in figure 1.4. As you can see, *judging* is related to *thinking* (air) and *feeling* (water). Yet, feeling and thinking are of a different polarity. The same situation is illustrated as *perceiving* causes a polarity to take place between *sensation* (earth) and *intuition* (fire).

potential, will remain predominant through life in one's views and reactions.

In psychology, the continually developing function of consciousness most important for our view of the world is called the superior function. Analogous to this is the superior function in astrology. Thus, in Fred's horoscope that element is earth, both in potential (sign) and circumstance (house), while in Marilyn

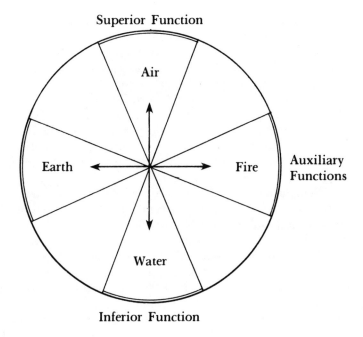

Figure 1.6. The gray areas between the functions illustrates how the functions mix. The area between air and earth, for example, provides the air-earth type. In this figure you can see that there is never a mixture of conflicting elements because they cannot share the gray middle area. When one function is conscious, the contradictory function is always in the unconscious. Planets in the unconscious element will always react from the unconscious part of the psyche. The remaining two elements can help the conscious function, but these need to be developed, as they belong half to the conscious and half to the unconscious.

Monroe's horoscope the superior element is air. The elements earth and air respectively had already developed when they were young. Such a development takes the form of a progressive differentiation; in other words, the superior function distinguishes itself more and more from the other functions because we can work with it more easily and clearly. The element then works so naturally that we are not even aware that we are acting typically for that element. An air type, for instance, will automatically approach everything through thinking.

In contrast to the obviously developed superior function, there is another function or element connected with the unconscious area of the psyche and therefore outside the mastery of the will and the conscious mind. This function we call inferior; astrologically, it is represented by an element opposite in direction to the superior element. If fire is the superior element, then earth is the inferior. If air is the superior element, then water is the inferior, etc. In Fred's horoscope, the earth element is superior; it follows then that the fire element is connected with the unconscious. The planets located in fire signs therefore work in his horoscope out of the unconscious: Jupiter in Aries and Pluto in Leo.

Being associated with the unconscious, Pluto symbolizes a part of the human psyche that by its very nature cannot be controlled by the conscious mind. Yet it is important to know that Pluto is part of the inferior or unconscious element, since Pluto can express itself in the psyche in various ways; for instance, a desire for power or show of power, mental showdowns, contests, and the like. If Pluto is located in an inferior element, that person will have great difficulty becoming conscious of those traits in himself. Moreover, it is characteristic of unconscious contents that they can break through into consciousness at the most inconvenient moments and cause disturbances. This calm and sensitive earth-water type can suddenly show a tough, fighting spirit and stubbornly stand his own ground, to the amazement of those who don't know him intimately.

In this context, it is also important to know that the psyche always strives for balance and that the unconscious has a compensating function in regard to the conscious mind. In practice, the stronger the consciousness and the stronger one's self-image, the stronger the unconscious will counteract these functions. The degree to which these counteractions act as a jamming station depends on the readiness of the conscious mind to digest or integrate such impulses. When we have two strongly occupied opposing elements in a horoscope, as one develops into a superior element the other will necessarily become the inferior element. In such a case, if the inferior element is just as strongly occupied, the unconscious counteractions are powerful and keep the conscious side under pressure.

In Marilyn Monroe's horoscope, we see the air element located opposite a strongly occupied but impersonal water element. Yet, the influence that evolves within the water element forms a powerful opposition for consciousness in different ways. When such a polarity becomes too strong, then compulsive actions due to the inferior element can appear, entirely escaping the person's awareness. With a strong air-water polarity, and air the superior element, one would perceive his world from a rational structure. Because of his strong water element he would also be fascinated by the illogical, the emotional and the most sentimental. Bouts of emotionalism, the irrational feeling that there is something missing in all that rationality, or sentimentally being in love, are all ways the water element can show itself. It gnaws on the foundation of the structure one identifies with (in this case the element air) and leaves behind a feeling of doubt and uncertainty.

We often see such a person attempting to reinforce the conscious structure. He begins to wonder why things are going a certain way, tries to contain the world within more rigid thought patterns, and becomes even less flexible as a result. This increasing rigidity of consciousness evokes even stronger unconscious reactions. The conscious mind is overwhelmed more forcefully with incomprehensible feelings, until a crisis helps achieve a state of balance between the unconscious and the conscious. This balance often doesn't happen until the complete inadequacy of the structure in all its facets is experienced and accepted. Persons with such a division of functions don't actually steer their lives with their conscious minds, but in reality live through their inferior functions. In the case of Marilyn Monroe this is the element water. Hence the following remarks of C.A. Meier:

> ...the function which is inferior per definition often is much more noticeable than the differentiated. Especially

in a thinking type an uncertain and precarious emotional life can strike us much sooner than his thinking, which is beyond reproach.[13]

In many cases, strangely enough, the fire element gets upset about material things, whereas earth, specifically oriented to concrete life, doesn't see anything wrong. Such a situation occurs when the fire element is strongly occupied (containing the Sun and the Moon, for instance), but the earth element influences the personal contents (for instance, Mercury and Ascendant in earth). When fire is superior, the element earth is directed toward security, and can unleash powerful counteractions from the unconscious— especially when fire has a great need for freedom and wild adventures. A businessman with this element division can plan the most fantastic schemes from behind his desk, but when it comes to actualizing them, he must play for security if he doesn't want sleepless nights.

Another example of a fire type with earth contradictions is the statement, "I would like to work part-time so I could have more free time for myself, but then I'd have to have at least $50,000 in reserve in my bank account!" An astrologer could explain this statement by referring to the earth content of the horoscope, without bringing in the conscious-unconscious division. By leaving out the principal characteristics of the superior and inferior functions, one only recognizes the existence of factors colored by a certain element, while the functioning of these factors within the psyche remains completely unclear. One can't determine in this way the origin of compulsive actions which can only be associated with unconscious impulses. The conscious mind, controlled by the will, doesn't need to be compulsive; when we are up against the incomprehensible, uncontrollable unconscious, we *do* feel this need.

In addition, the polarity between the superior and the inferior function gives a much greater depth to the development of a person's motives. Now we can discern how much a person really wants certain things and on which points he is so sensitive that he will lose control at the slightest excuse. Moreover, what Toni Wolff says is all too true.

[13]Meier, C.A., *Bewusstsein*, p. 138.

> ...the problem of the opposition of the types is often...the real though unconscious cause of a neurosis, and this problematical question is therefore also the problem that plays the greatest role in such cases at the beginning of psychological analysis.[14]

So far we have discussed the horoscopes of adults who already have worked out part of their circumstances and to whom we can relate the total horoscope. A child lives up to his potential (planets in the signs) much more than he does according to circumstances (planets in the houses). His protected environment guards against extremes in circumstance, with a few exceptions. A great difference between potential and circumstance could contribute to a certain amount of tension. For instance, a fire planet in an earth house demands greater adjustment to the demands of circumstance than that same planet in an air or water house.

Tension can arise within the element division in many ways:

a) Two opposing elements appear most important in the element division as a whole. If one of these elements becomes superior, the other can only express itself through the language of the unconscious.

b) The total division can seem harmonious, but that doesn't necessarily imply stability. The various planets making up this totality can be forced to express themselves in strange territory; for instance, the Sun in an air sign that is expressed through a water house. This polarity between potential and circumstance can give rise to ultimately developing another function into our chief function, whereby the actual potential becomes suppressed. Upbringing and other circumstances can play a great role here, though this doesn't necessarily lead to something as radical as a change of superior function.

c) A certain element can be completely lacking, both in potential and circumstance. Not having the contents of that element nor feeling the need to direct energy in those areas of life indicated by that element doesn't hinder the person. Whether life will run

---

[14]Wolff, T., See footnote 1, p. 64.

smoothly or not in those areas depends upon the rest of the horoscope (aspects, relations between the houses, etc.). I would like to emphasize that a missing element doesn't necessarily mean that one feels hindered, as normal function is possible. (In some cases the environment can be more troubled by the missing element than the person himself!)

d) A certain element can be represented in potential (sign) without having any way of expressing itself in circumstance (house). In such a case, the contents (planets) have a more difficult time coming into their own right. The need for expression becomes more acute as more personal contents are involved: for instance, having the Sun, Mercury, and Ascendant in earth signs, with earth houses empty. Then there is a stronger possibility of developing into another function type for which a distinct potential exists.

e) A certain element is not present in potential (by sign) but appears in circumstance (by house). In such a case, the experiences of life can bring about changes in character, even though that may not happen easily. Having no planets in air signs, but having planets in air houses means, for instance, that social traits are not very strong in potential, but they can be refined through contacts with friends, acquaintances, or a partner. (Take the rest of the horoscope into consideration, of course.)

f) Some horoscopes show such a broad element distribution that the astrologer can barely make a choice. That means the person in question may have difficulty developing the superior function. For instance, someone with Sun in Aries, Moon in Taurus, Mercury in Pisces and a Libra Ascendant won't have an easy youth, due to the inner contradictions. Four important personal contents in four different elements mean that one important personal content will always act from the unconscious, as I mentioned at the beginning of this section. (In such cases, I have often found that the element in which the Sun is located becomes important, or in any case plays an important role.)

5. SUPERIOR AND INFERIOR ELEMENT:
POSSIBILITIES AND DIFFICULTIES

In the last section we discussed the relationship between the inferior and superior functions. We assumed that one element will clearly crystallize, but in practice, this is not always the case. When two non-opposing elements both play an important role in consciousness, each containing personal contents, this can produce a mixed type that has characteristics from both. Eventually, the balance usually falls to one element and the second element then plays an important auxiliary function. Of course, this cannot be the case with opposing elements such as air-water and fire-earth! There can never be a mixed type formed from two elements in which one is inferior by definition and operates from the unconscious. The division of the elements with its emphasis on the personal planets primarily says something about our *consciousness*. We show this schematically in figure 1.7. Imagine that earth is the superior function. Then by necessity fire is located in the unconscious. The two remaining elements—air and water—can develop as auxiliary functions.

Fred's horoscope has the element division shown in figure 1.7. Earth is superior, fire inferior. Being strongly occupied, the element water soon becomes auxiliary and remains subordinate to the

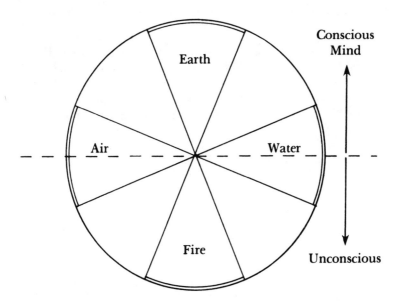

Figure 1.7. The element division in Fred's horoscope. Here Earth is the superior function while Fire becomes inferior. The Air and Water facets of self develop as auxiliary functions.

element earth in expression, but the water characteristics can be seen in Fred's conscious mentality and his behavior. We can call him an earth-water type, with an emphasis on earth.

In Marilyn Monroe's horoscope (see page 18), it isn't as easy to select a second element since she was predominantly an air type with strong unconscious emotional reactions from the element water. Auxiliary functions could only be formed by the elements fire and earth, neither of these being contrary to air, her superior function.

Though much has been written about the constructive side of the inferior function, there still seems to be an aversion or fear in many people regarding the concerns of that element, as though it were something we shouldn't actually possess. It is difficult for us to imagine that a function posing so many problems for our consciousness can also be constructive, can even be our salvation in certain difficult psychological situations. One of the clearest descriptions of the inferior element's function, or (psychologically speaking) the inferior function itself, is to be found in *Lectures on Jung's Typology* by Marie-Louise von Franz and James Hillman. M.-L. von Franz sketches for us the following role of the inferior function.[15]

...The inferior function is the door through which all the figures of the unconscious come into consciousness. Our conscious realm is like a room with four doors, and the fourth door by which the Shadow[16], the Animus[17] or the Anima and the personification of the Self[18] come in.

[15]von Franz, M.-L., "The inferior function," p. 54, in von Franz, M.-L., & J. Hillman, *Lectures on Jung's Typology*, Spring Verlag, Zürich, 1971.

[16]Seen individually, the "shadow" represents the "personal darkness," the meanings of our psyche during our lifetime that are not admitted or are rejected or repressed. Seen collectively, the shadow represents the general dark side in the human being, the structural tendency towards darkness and inferiority, that every person has within him. Becoming conscious of our inferior function often causes a confrontation with the shadow connected with it. See Jacobi, J., *The Psychology of C.G. Jung*, Routledge & Kegan Paul, London, 1973, pp. 109-114.

[17]The concepts *Anima* and *Animus* may become more clear when we consider Jung's example: every Adam has within him his Eve (anima) and every Eve her own Adam (animus). Each person seeks to encounter someone who resembles the inner Adam or Eve in order to remain psychologically in balance. From: Lievegoed, B.M., *De Levensloope van de mens*, Rotterdam, 1978, p. 90.

They do not enter as often through the other doors, which is in a way self-evident: the inferior function is so close to the unconscious and remains so barbaric and inferior and undeveloped that it is naturally the weak spot in consciousness through which the figures of the unconscious can break in. In consciousness it is experienced as a weak spot, as that disagreeable thing which will never leave one in peace and always causes trouble. Every time one feels he has acquired a certain inner balance, a firm standpoint, something happens from within or without to throw it over again. This force always comes through the fourth door, which cannot be shut. The other three doors of the inner room can be closed. But on the fourth door the lock does not work, and there, when one is least prepared for it, the unexpected will come in again. Thank God, one might add, for otherwise the whole life process would petrify and stagnate in a wrong kind of consciousness. The inferior function is the ever-bleeding wound of the conscious personality, but through it the unconscious can always come in and so enlarge consciousness and bring forth a new attitude.

As long as one has not developed the other functions, the two auxiliary functions, they too will be open doors. In a person who has only developed one superior function, the two auxiliary functions will operate in the same way as the inferior function and will appear in personifications of the Shadow, the Animus and the Anima. When one has succeeded in developing three functions, in locking three of the inner doors, the problem of the fourth door still remains, for that is the one that is apparently meant not to be locked. There one has to succumb, one has to suffer defeat in order to develop further...

---

[18]The Self is the center of our psychic totality, just as the *I* is the center of our consciousness. The Self contains both the conscious and the unconscious parts of the psyche. See Jacobi, J., *The Psychology of C.G. Jung*, Routledge & Kegan Paul, London, 1973, p. 107.

This doesn't sound very pleasant to the conscious mind, yet the conscious mind is but a part of our total psyche. Even people who know Jung's typology don't necessarily know which type they actually are. This fact confronts us with the paradox that the conscious mind isn't necessarily as conscious as it seems, according to Edward C. Whitmont.[19] He also says that a person belongs to a certain type when the function of that type is the most developed and differentiated. Whether he is conscious of this or not is another question, as one's orientation often begins in childhood without conscious choice. Whitmont also states:

> ...It cannot be stressed enough that the inferior function is inferior because of insufficient development rather than deficient capacity. A feeling type is perfectly capable of thinking; he just will not bother to do it. Consequently he habitually and automatically takes notice only of his feelings. The thinking type is capable of feeling but it happens in spite of him, more often than not. He does not do the feeling, it does *him*, in the form of unconscious emotion...[20]

Whitmont's last point, as we stated earlier, is one of the characteristics of the inferior function, and therefore our consciousness has no grasp on it and cannot steer it. The conscious mind only experiences the inferior element's way of expression in arbitrary moments—often when it is inconvenient! The inferior element has still more characteristic features and ways of manifesting itself which can be listed as follows:

a) The inferior function, in contrast with the conscious mind, is relatively undeveloped, thus reacting in an elementary manner. This manner of acting is called "archaic."

b) The reactions of the inferior function are slow and can hardly be speeded up, even after much practice. The inferior function demands our time, something in short supply in our Western

---

[19]Whitmont, E.C., *The Symbolic Quest: Basic Concepts of Analytical Psychology*, Princeton University Press, Princeton, 1969, p. 153.

[20]*Ibid*, p. 154-155.

culture. M.-L. von Franz[21] gave the example of a girlfriend with an inferior earth function. Shopping with her for a blouse was an ordeal; the whole store had to be turned upside down and still her friend could not make a choice. Her inferior function (sensation) works very slowly, as all inferior functions do. That is why we become annoyed with that part of our psyche. The slow reaction of the inferior element is helpful in some regard, however; through that slowness the unconscious has a chance to penetrate the conscious mind and do its work. A confrontation can take place. All the time the girlfriend was busy buying a blouse—an earth function—her superior fire function was temporarily switched off, even though it would grab the reins again soon enough. All kinds of contents in herself, of which she was unaware, could enter her consciousness through the process of buying a blouse. This gives her the possibility of recognizing certain dormant character traits and/or faculties, even though recognition may come later when one reflects upon the experience.

That same slowness of the inferior function also means that we would rather avoid that element or function, for we are accustomed to the much quicker reactions of the superior function. Therefore, the inferior function is not called in right away. The quicker superior function continually takes the lead when reacting to information, even though the situation may require an entirely different approach than that function is suited for. For instance, ask a thinking type what he is feeling, as M.-L. von Franz suggests, and he will answer with a mental idea or a conventional silencer. If you really press the point he will become embarrassed, not having any idea what he actually feels. He can think for hours about that!

c) As we saw earlier, the consciousness cannot use the inferior function as a foundation. It comes and goes at its own pleasure; the power of our will does not reach the area of our inferior element. To refer again to the feeling type; naturally he can think—often thinking long and deeply—and can achieve quite a bit on this level. But despite all the knowledge he possesses, and the fact that he can think adequately, at critical moments he may not be able to

[21]See footnote 15, p. 8.

command his mental function and might, for instance, fail an examination he otherwise could have passed easily.

d) The inferior element shows the area where we are vulnerable. This Achilles heel manifests itself through those things to which we are vulnerable, and which we find hard to bear, thus causing us to react in an emotional way. The inferior element eludes our grasp, giving us the feeling of not being able to control or protect that side of ourselves, and therefore it can be very tricky or prone to overcompensation. When our inferior element comes into play, the least incident can unbalance us and we react in a childish, oversensitive or insecure way. We can even unconsciously and unwillingly terrorize our surroundings: others walk around on tiptoe, afraid of another irrational outburst and finding it absolutely impossible to talk to us at the time.

e) The inferior element connects our conscious and unconscious, which is of great importance for maintaining or repairing psychic balance. Through the unconscious, we adapt to our own psychic totality, just as through the superior function our conscious-ness adapts to the outside world. The compensating function of the unconscious is the motor which maintains our conscious life. To this end, the unconscious has its own language and its own mechanism. Once these mechanisms appear strange to the conscious mind, we will examine the unconscious more closely.

6. MECHANISMS OF THE UNCONSCIOUS

Dreams, daydreams and fantasies are the most important mechan-isms we can use to become aware of our unconscious. Dreams may suggest what is going on in the unconscious of the individual, even when consciousness has no knowledge of this, but also when something has already penetrated through to consciousness. For example, in our daydreams we may continually play the role of an unconquerable figure for whom nothing is impossible and who always makes things turn out all right. This can be an unconscious compensation for an attitude and pattern in life that is much less impressive. Feelings of inadequacy, failure, lack of ability, and anxieties from our daily lives can call forth counterparts in our dream world, without our being directly aware of these anxieties or even remembering what we were daydreaming about. It happens without any effort from our conscious mind, and compensates for the outer situation. Becoming conscious of the contents of our dreams, daydreams and fantasies can help us become aware of our outer situation so we can do something about it, within our ability.

If we do not pay attention to dream indications, the unconscious has other ways of manifesting itself, ranging from seemingly minor slips of the tongue or forgetfulness, to the development of serious neuroses. Though the conscious mind experiences this as highly unpleasant, the resulting tension will press upon consciousness in order that the disturbed balance between the conscious and unconscious be restored, allowing the psyche to balance itself.

The forms of expression used by the unconscious are very specific: the unconscious speaks a language of images, as in our dreams. Like the irrational part of the "primitive" spirit, it precedes, lies beyond, or transcends reason. Expression through imagery is one of the most specific characteristics of the unconscious. Mental contents and processes can be represented in imagery, for instance, as figures and events. Thoughts and feelings appear in the guise of persons who speak them or act them out. Moods can be expressed by images of landscape, instincts by animals, etc. At some level, each individual knows his own specific images. One person will feel a deep melancholy seeing a leaf fall from a tree, while another person may not even *see* the leaf fall, but in turn will experience the same sort of melancholy gazing at a seascape.

The forms of unconscious expression always penetrate consciousness without being influenced or changed by it. These manifestations, therefore, are pure and original, undifferentiated to a great extent. Our consciousness takes in the everyday course of events. We learn to use a function or element better and better, as it refines its expression through use. In contrast, the inferior function residing in the unconscious stays in an undeveloped condition; we cannot or will not deal with it. On its own, it sometimes breaks through into consciousness. The possibility of developing or refining itself in this way is slight, so this element remains active in its original state. Therefore, the inferior function is called primitive, because it is simple, undeveloped and original. The word primitive is loaded with negative prejudice in our time and the word "archaic" reflects its meaning more objectively.

In someone with the thinking function as the main expression of consciousness, the feeling function (water element) will express itself in an archaic manner. Though he can set everything he sees and hears into neat, orderly rows in his thought world, sometimes such deep and elusive feelings well up that he feels completely overwhelmed. Sometimes he lets himself be swept away by them, even into sentimentality. He cannot steer his feelings nor understand why the calm, balanced thinker can suddenly come under the spell of emotions and feelings. We can cite the well-known example of the professor in the film *The Blue Angel*. During the day, he was a rigid, straight professor and a disciplinarian with his students, while at night he was the helpless victim of a nightclub performer. She could inflame him by setting loose his inferior feeling function. She only misused him, and the manner in which he allowed himself to be completely bowled over into a world of dreams existing for him alone clearly shows the archaic and in some ways childish character of his feeling function.

When a certain element can be singled out as being the inferior element, such as fire in Fred's horoscope and water in Marilyn Monroe's, then the planets located in these elements will express themselves in an archaic way, not influenced by consciousness. This does not mean these planets will express themselves in a negative manner. It is true that these planets are connected with the counteractions of our unconscious and the conscious mind isn't always thankful later. Nonetheless, these planets can give us a helping hand through their activity whenever our consciousness runs away with us. Often, these planets correct us and show that we hold ourselves too rigidly within the bounds of our conscious mind, which is still limited and rather one-sided.

A strongly intuitive (fire) type with Venus in earth can be capable of a permanent relationship, despite his search for possibilities, freedom, and basic truths. The earth element compels him to search for security in the area of love. The partner helps this otherwise fiery individual stand more firmly, with two feet on the ground. Inwardly, the fire type will have some difficulty with this restriction of his freedom. Still, in connection with the unconscious, his earth Venus produces both an inner tension and eventually a greater inner balance, no matter how contrary that may sound. How far these conscious and unconscious contents collide with or fulfill each other depends upon the individual's self-awareness, and that in turn depends on how much he can accept himself with all his imperfections and possibilities.

It is striking how many people fall in love with their opposite type, though we would say at first glance that they do not belong together at all. Yet, such radically different attitudes of consciousness do not have to lead to a split; on the contrary, such relationships are often very creative because one represents the unconscious of the other. The "language" spoken by their contrasting superior elements is so at variance, however, that when the people involved do not see this difference, conflicts can result.

It will be evident by now that the division of elements is of great importance for the foundation of the horoscope; also that the tension between opposite elements in the human psyche as well as between people is not necessarily negative. This tension may give rise to creativity. It cannot be denied that tension within a horoscope coming from the division of elements may cause frustration, yet I would rather call this creative frustration: the driving motive behind all of our actions comes from this very division.

7. Examples of Element Division Interpretation

When we begin the interpretation of a horoscope, the element division gives us a first impression. It is a general scheme that can be used as a reference for a more refined interpretation. Taking Fred's horoscope on page 14 as an example, we have found that earth plays the main role, followed by water. On this basis, we can say the following about his hosorcope:

Fred's consciousness is directed towards a concrete perception of facts and phenomena and their practical and material value. His views are based on a sober, everyday reality. In such a reality, everything has a concrete and tangible form, inspiring a sense of security, and he will feel completely comfortable with himself. In the concrete and material realm, he can express himself very well. His feeling for form and proportion is well-developed so he can be creative in this respect without much effort. Besides having a practical, patient nature he has a fairly directed way of spending his energy, going about his work and hobbies in an efficient and diligent manner. He has a feeling for work situations, conditions, and relations, and this is strengthened by his well developed water element that fulfills his superior earth element in many respects.

Because of the combination of earth and water, he needs a feeling of loyalty and union in order to develop his earth characteristics: perseverance, solidarity and reliability. Due to the passive nature of both elements, this man unmistakably needs stimulation from his surroundings, family, friends, or wife to motivate him. Although he is perfectly contented by himself, due to the strong water element, his self-image is largely derived from what he can mean to other people. His attitude is predominantly turned inward, and consequently we can say that he is rather reserved. His inner life is strongly developed, making him vulnerable and overly sensitive. Because his consciousness is primarily directed to the perceptible world, supplemented by a feeling evaluation of what he sees and experiences, the abstract and theoretical belong to his weaker side. It is sometimes difficult for him to place facts and phenomena in a broader frame of reference, though he will have a good view of the facts as such.

Since his superior element is earth, the fire in his horoscope will produce counteractions now and then. Concepts such as *change* and *possibility* are central to fire and, seen in the light of his underdeveloped fire planets, Fred will have difficulty with change and a skeptical attitude toward new developments. Possibly he is anxious about change, and will approach any new possibility negatively, as for instance: "I won't succeed in than anyway, or, what *can't* go wrong!"

The here and now, the concrete and tangible, form the reality to which he limits himself. As a result, he will focus on concrete pleasures, not so much raw sensuality but more the enjoyment of having extra money for good clothes, luxury items, furnishings for his house, good food, in short, everything pleasurable or comfortable. A fire type—disregarding the rest of the horoscope!—can live for years in a bare, unpainted room without even noticing.

Looking again at Fred's horoscope, it will now be clear that the trine aspect between the Moon in Pisces and his Scorpio Ascendant is very important for his consciousness, as this aspect is formed by two water signs, the element playing such an important role for his consciousness. In contrast, the conflict arising from fire to earth through the Pluto in Leo square the Sun and Mars in Taurus can be more detrimental than we might assume from the conventional interpretation of the aspects. In this horoscope, earth is the main element, which means that these signs squaring each other are at the same time opposing each other as superior and inferior element. If they had been two auxiliary functions there might still have been a fire-earth conflict, but for Fred's consciousness this would have been less acute.

As another example, the opposition between Saturn in Virgo and Moon in Pisces is also very important for Fred's consciousness. Again the aspect is formed from the superior element (earth), but now with an auxiliary element (water). In contrast, the trine aspect between Venus in Gemini and Neptune in Libra will work from the unconscious parts of the psyche since the element air, where this aspect is found, is not one of Fred's conscious functions. With an earth-water combination, the fire and air elements will work from the unconscious. The air element can still develop in a later stage, since it has an auxiliary function and is not in conflict with the superior element. In this way, according to the effect of the aspects, we can bring about a differentiation, a first step toward a more selective approach to reading the aspects.

The conclusions about Marilyn Monroe's horoscope are similar. Her chart appears on page 18. Here again, one element plays the main role—in this case, air. As a result, water is fated to become an inferior element. Marilyn's conscious attitude was a rational and theoretical approach to facts and events; relating people, facts, and abstract thoughts to one another took a primary place. The generally harmonious and mediating behavior of an air type can give the impression of "trimming one's sail to the wind." Her intellectual capacities joined with her flexibility of thought, word and gesture, and she was able to communicate, to make contacts, and handle herself easily in social situations.

She continually tried to arrange everything into neat little cubicles in her own mental world picture, adjusting her own theories and beliefs accordingly. Through this, she ran the risk, despite her obvious social skills, of alienating people around her. With this strong an air emphasis, there is also a good possibility that she would create an unreal, abstract dream world in which everything has its place, without feeling compelled to try out these theories in reality. Any person with this element breakdown could build a personal world that is so mental in nature that she would make a definitely cool or perhaps emotionless impression on others.

At this point the unconscious element, water, could either come to her aid or undermine her. The planets Pluto, Saturn, Mars and Uranus, located in water signs, played an important role. Her emotional life was unable to develop because of her rationally-oriented consciousness. It created a strong pull and exerted an intense pressure on her consciousness, emerging now and then into her consciousness with sudden explosions. Earlier we stated that the psyche continually strives for balance. The presence of air in this horoscope is so dominant that the counteractions from the unconscious water element would have to be just as powerful.

The inferior element always works suddenly; it rears its head at the most unexpected moments. This lack of control is reinforced by the location of Uranus in a water sign. Saturn was also located in a water sign (Scorpio), which often indicates a slowed reaction from the unconscious, which, once it has broken through, can persist for a long time. Moreover, Saturn, indicating feelings of responsibility and a sense of perseverance, cannot be easily directed in the inaccessible unconscious. She could run into difficulty through her perseverance in affairs bound to fail or by taking responsibility either too seriously, or not seriously enough. Once she was emotionally committed to something, she went all out for it. The location of a planet in an unconscious element, therefore, does not have a necessarily negative meaning.

Mars in a woman's horoscope usually indicates the image she carries of her husband or male partner (called the *Animus* in Jungian psychology). Marilyn's Mars in Pisces could cause all kinds of difficulties from the inferior element unless she was extremely cautious in her love affairs and sexuality. In fact, she needed to be careful in every aspect of her emotional life, having the inclination, just as the professor in *The Blue Angel*, to give in to drives in herself which she couldn't fully understand.

The strong duality between the element air, so filled with personal planets, and the element water, strongly occupied by impersonal planets, created a strong tension in her character which manifested itself as an adaption primarily to the outer life and a lack of adaptation to the inner. The fire element, indicated by the Leo

Ascendant, served as a refuge; she could surrender herself more and more to new possibilities, she could wander further with her thoughts, just like a fire sign would and she could create a fantasy future no one else could enter.[22]

The element tension in Marilyn Monroe's horoscope is greater than Fred's, even though air is strong both in potential (signs) and in circumstance (houses), something that appears so promising at first glance. On one hand, Marilyn applied all her communicative, connective and intellectual capacities with success, but the overly strong emphasis on air in this non-conflicting way automatically put the counter-element of water under a disproportionate amount of pressure. Here it was not the conscious mind that was in conflict, but rather the unconscious that was disharmonious with the conscious mind. To some degree this is always true, yet in this case an unusual amount of tension was involved. The rest of the contents of the horoscope should be viewed in this light.

Finally, one more example: Peter. See Chart 3 on page 42. This horoscope has the element division shown in figure 1.8. Peter's horoscope stands out because of its broad distribution. The Aries Sun and the Leo Ascendant are in fire, and the Taurus Moon and M.C. as personal contents are in the opposite element of earth. In air, we find Venus in Aquarius and Mars in Gemini, in water we

Element	Signs	Houses	Total
FIRE	☉ ♇ Asc.	—	3
EARTH	☽ Mc. ♄	☽ ♄ ♂ ♀	7
AIR	♂ ♇ ♀ ♃	♇ ♃ ♄	7
WATER	♄ ☿	☿ ☉ ♇	5

Figure 1.8. The element division for Peter, Chart 3.

[22]An astrologer would never be able to predict from the horoscope alone the degree to which this will happen in the person's life, but he could certainly indicate the danger and know that it plays a certain role.

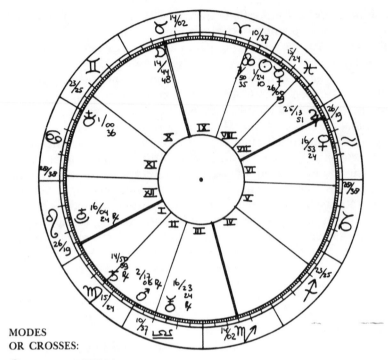

**MODES
OR CROSSES:**

(6) Cardinal: ☉♅♂♄/♃☽

(11) Fixed: ☽MC☿Asc♀♃/♄☿♇♅

(5) Mutable: ♄☿/♅♀♇

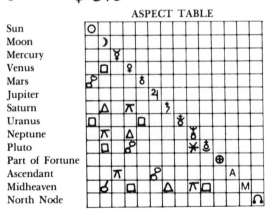

ASPECT TABLE

	Sun	Moon	Mercury	Venus	Mars	Jupiter	Saturn	Uranus	Neptune	Pluto	Part of Fortune	Ascendant	Midheaven	North Node
Sun	☉													
Moon		☽												
Mercury			☿											
Venus		□		♀										
Mars	♂			☌										
Jupiter					☍	♃								
Saturn		△	⊼			⚹	♄							
Uranus	□						⚻	♅						
Neptune		⊼	△					☌	♆					
Pluto	□		☍					⚹	⚹	♇				
Part of Fortune										⊕				
Ascendant		⊼		☍							A			
Midheaven		☌	□		△		⊼□					M		
North Node													☊	

ELEMENTS:

Fire: (3)
♌ ☊
Asc

Earth: (2)
♄ MC
♃

Air: (2)
☍ ☿ ♅
♀

Water: (5)
♅ ♀
♇ ☉ ☽

find Mercury in Pisces, a placement not to be underestimated. In short, there is something in every element, and at first glance it seems difficult to make out what is dominant. Experience has taught me that in such a case the Sun, the Ascendant, and Mercury are especially important. The Sun plays an important role, particularly in childhood. In Peter's horoscope the Sun is in fire, not conflicting with Mercury in Pisces, following the division of elements. In practice, Peter does seem to view the world from the fire element. With the passage of years, however, some change has gradually taken place. In the horoscope this is indicated by the rather strong fire potential in personal contents (signs) contrasted with the complete lack of fire circumstances (houses). Though air and earth signs are most strongly represented numerically, this does not mean these elements are the most important for consciousness. Earth is important because the Moon is located in it, both by sign (Taurus) and circumstance (being in the tenth house), while Venus and Mars also appear in earth houses. Water, on the other hand, has a lower numerical value, but we find Mercury there in both sign and house. The Sun is in the eighth house. Thereby, water has a good relationship with the element of consciousness, fire, while earth is contradictory to fire. This assures that fire and water will play an important role, certainly in the first part of life. See Chart 3.

Strong counter-reactions come from earth and to a lesser degree from air, making his base shaky. There is a chance that Peter will take a different course than would be indicated by the Sun: there are no fire house placements while earth as a whole is very strong. This implies a couple of possibilities. First, he can escape into the function reflected by the water element to reduce the tension between fire and earth, and slowly make that into his superior function (unconsciously of course). A second possibility is that at a certain point in his life, he makes a temporary or permanent reversal and lets the element earth become the superior function. It may sound somewhat simple, changing from one function to the other, but in practice this often involves a number of crises, where one is

---

Chart 3. Peter was born on March 22, 1950 at Lisse, Holland, at 3:30 pm. The data is supplied from his birth certificate. House system is Placidus. Chart used with permission.

forced to see one's shortcomings through neurotic symptoms. With such a broad distribution where the elements of both the Sun and Ascendant are unable to give form to circumstance, it is possible that the element is exchanged in one's lifetime, with turbulent results. Fire and earth always remain a polarity, and his Sun will show itself from an angle which, astrologically, is directly contradictory to the one presented by his Moon.

Air is least occupied by sign (potential) and even less occupied by house (circumstance). From this, we may conclude that logical, abstract thinking is not Peter's strongest side; he probably will not have much need for it. His emotional life (water element), on the other hand, will play a continually greater role for him, perhaps helping him develop into an entirely different person in the course of his life.

In Peter's horoscope, the square aspect between Venus in Aquarius and the Moon in Taurus (as well as the other Venus and Moon aspects) will initially be active in his unconscious. Considering the ever-developing emotional content, this is apparently contradictory since the Moon and Venus have always been considered planets that rule (or symbolize) the emotions. To prevent any confusion, we should bear in mind the following difference: the division of the elements shows which element is characteristic for the *manner* in which one approaches the world. The planets are energies and indicate more the *contents* of that energy than a manner of approach. For instance, someone with water as superior element sees everything around him through his emotional faculty, yet that does not necessarily imply that he is warm and sensitive. This is decided by the planets. Returning to Peter's horoscope, though we can say fire will be of importance in his youth, it does not follow that it will remain so at a later age. On the contrary, the distribution shows a number of tensions that can manifest themselves during crises and cause sudden reversals. Fire remains his strongest element in *potential*; this implies that he will never be able to refine nor differentiate any new main function as well as he does his actual superior function.

The division of the elements in itself is a very important feature of the horoscope which will be clearer when we relate it to the division of the crosses. We will deal with this more thoroughly in the following chapter and see how they can be combined in Chapter Three.

Chapter Two

The Crosses:
Activity and Direction of Psychic Energy

1. The Concept of Energy in Psychology

The introduction of the concept *energy* into psychology and astrology makes it possible for us to see separate psychic phenomena in a functional relationship to each other. It makes it possible to distinguish processes within a nearly inextricable dynamic reaction as if we were dealing with static data.

The concept *psychic energy* has been consciously borrowed from physics, and its place in psychology was analogous in the beginning. In certain respects, the general laws of physics can be applied to psychic energy, although psychological investigations have repeatedly shown deviations from the traditonal meaning and processes of physics. As a result, the concept *psychic energy* has gradually begun to lead an independent existence. Mainly, these deviations are due to the fact that we are not dealing with lifeless material but with the intricate human psyche, in which a complex of factors influence the progress of the psychic processes.[1]

One of the most important correspondences is that energy can only flow when inequalities or differences within the psyche cause a kind of *fall*. Just as water keeps moving as the river flows from high to low, so the psychic current depends upon differences in *charge* between psychic contents. We cannot grasp physical energy itself, we only know it through its manner of manifestation. Similarly, we

[1]Wolff, T., *Studien zu C.G. Jungs Psychologie*, Rhein Verlag, Zurich, 1959, p. 174.

can only observe psychic energy through its specific patterns of expression and reaction. Studying these can give deeper insight into the way psychic energy moves.

The psyche functions as an independent totality, adapting both to outward conditions and to inner structural specifics of the individual. Just as moral, ethical, social and cultural values can change radically in a short period, so can inner values change as one grows older. Every phase of life brings with it special psychological circumstances, needs, and wants. This interaction of the psyche with the continually changing inner and outer values makes the psyche one large dynamic system.[2] Psychic energy keeps everything going in this system, whether the individual likes the way this takes place or not.

In the preceding chapter we saw the importance of the division of the psyche into conscious and unconscious sections. Jung went a step further and divided the unconscious as follows:

> *The personal unconscious* (the top level of the unconscious): stored there are all the contents which can be made conscious or which once were conscious. These are the things we have forgotten, repressed, and didn't want to recall, as well as our own complexes and hidden talents, which lie dormant in this part of the unconscious.

> *The collective unconscious* (the deeper levels of the unconscious): these levels never have and never will become conscious. What is contained here is the universally human, without any personal tinge. All inherited reaction patterns, all primitive human contents are present in this level. This part of the human psyche connects an individual with every other human being and is the source of motifs shared the world over. The collective unconscious is sometimes also called the objective psyche in Jungian psychology. No longer being connected with personal and thus subjective values, it reacts

---

[2]For more information concerning phases of life see: Hamaker-Zondag, K.M., *Astro-Psychology*, Aquarian Press, Wellingborough, 1980, Chapter 8; Lievegoed, B., De Levensloop van de mens. Ontwikkeling en Ontwikkelingsmogelijkheden in Verschillende Levensfasen, Rotterdam, 1978; Jung, C. G., "The Stages of Life," *Modern Man in Search of a Soul*, Routledge & Kegan Paul, London, 1933, pp. 109-131.

and works completely from the collective unconscious and universal human values.[3]

The psyche is always striving for balance, and psychic energy plays a key role in this. Whenever our consciousness receives too strong an emphasis, mechanisms of repression are overly activated, and the unconscious initiates compensating actions, completely beyond the control of the individual's will. When psychic energy has been concentrated too long in consciousness, characteristics dormant in the unconscious haven't had a chance for expression. This results in an inadequate ability to react in certain situations, and thus an inner need arises to bring this potential ability to the surface. The great difference in charge between consciousness and the unconscious results in a transfer of psychic energy to the unconscious. This happens, for instance, when someone continually uses his superior element at times when his inferior element would be better equipped to handle the situation. As the conscious constantly draws attention to itself, and the unconscious subsequently receives little or no energy or attention, a difference in charge gradually occurs. This continues until the deficiency of the inferior element is so great that it begins to draw energy back to itself. The connection between the conscious and the unconscious is formed by our inferior function.[4]

When the superior element is air, we tend to see everything from a mental viewpoint. We react to our surroundings with our minds, we communicate words rather than feelings. If air is the superior element, water is the inferior function, and will stay in the unconscious. Air will not handle emotional circumstances as easily as water would, so this individual may try to be logical or mental in an emotional situation. Too much energy is being put into the superior function, giving no energy to the unconscious water element. This may cause environmental problems, because the individual is not reacting to circumstances in a way that others will understand. Some may say this person is "cool." Or you may find

[3] For the most comprehensive information about the collective unconscious see Jung, C.G., *The Archetypes and the Collective Unconscious*, Collected Works, Vol. 9, Part 1, Routledge & Kegan Paul, London, 1975.

[4] Wolff, T., *Studien zu C. G. Jungs Psychologie*, Rhein Verlag, Zurich, 1959, p. 190.

this person talking at moments when tenderness is required. This causes psychic problems within the self, for sooner or later the unconscious will take the needed energy to itself, and the superior function will have to cope with unconscious pressures.

The example above shows the process of expression of psychic energy within time, in a series of events. However, if we examine the movement of psychic energy in the light of the psyche's totality, we can distinguish certain coordinated and simultaneous processes. The conscious-unconscious division of the psyche is the basis of *synchronic compensation*: *i.e.*, the phenomenon that, as certain conscious contents are lacking, there is a simultaneous increase in unconscious activity. (If the unconscious gets the upper hand, the conscious is functioning inadequately at the same time.)

One can speak of a division of powers within the whole. Through Freudian slips of the pen or tongue, our conscious notices an increase in independent unconscious activity and is eventually able to correct it. This correcting is a conscious *interference* to slow down the natural movement of psychic energy. Without interference, psychic energy would flow from where it is present to where there is a lack. A natural movement from full consciousness to the emptier unconscious would then take place. There is no law dictating that energy must first flow back into the unconscious until a static balance is achieved. On the contrary, Toni Wolff says, "...It is inherent to the creative nature of the psyche that intereference with the plain course of nature forms its structure."[5] This indicates that humans possess the possibility of influencing psychic processes in certain directions.

There are two different processes in the course of psychic energy:

A horizontal or *diachronic*[6] process that takes place in time and which is connected with a chronological order of events, and

A vertical or *synchronic*[7] process that relates to the transfer of psychic energy, i.e. the amount and the

[5]*Ibid*, p. 188.

[6]Diachronic means of or pertaining to the time of the earth's existence.

[7]Synchronic means a process in the spatial sense: more than one thing is happening at different levels at the same time.

direction of flow at any given moment between consciousness and the unconscious.

The direction and division of psychic energy at a certain
moment in the synchronic process is accompanied by a certain
attitude of consciousness. This attitude evokes reactions from both
the unconscious and the outside world. The nature of the unconscious implies that its reactions escape the conscious mind, yet,
mixed with the actions of consciousness, these reactions in turn
evoke counteractions from the outside world. These counteractions
are experienced as important incidents or events. These events in
turn have repercussions and influence the attitude of consciousness.
The flow of energy that consciousness demands is changed,
bringing another alteration in the unconscious and its reactions.
From events occurring chronologically in time, we can learn about
the nature and the extent of the interaction between the diachronic
process (horizontal in time) and the synchronic process (the vertical
transfer of energy in a more spatial sense) and therefore about the
relative amount of energy involved. Psychic energy is a time-space-
continuum, whereby independent events relate to each other within
the division between consciousness and the unconscious. Psychic
energy explains not so much the material form of expression as the
mutual relationship between psychic contents.

To give examples, everyone has said at times, "I used to be
interested in that, but now I've completely lost interest." Or, "I used
to feel more intensely or perceive things more sharply, but now I'm
indifferent." And applied in a more spatial sense, "I would really
like to do certain things, but in spite of my will power, I don't seem
to be able to bring up enough energy." This shows a first condition:
energy can neither originate from nothingness nor return to
nothingness; the total amount of energy in a closed system always
remains constant. In psychology, this condition means that energy
has withdrawn from a former investment and has now activated
another content, which may as yet be unknown to us.

In the second case, in spite of his will power, the person
in question can achieve nothing. Energy is not at the disposal of
consciousness, implying that this energy must be present somewhere
in the unconscious. Often we notice this by a more vivid dream life
or, where there are repressions and other psychic imbalances, we see
such symptoms as nervousness, restlessness, emotional irritability,

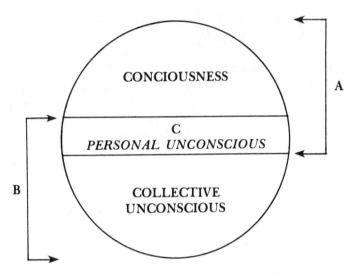

Figure 2.1. The personal unconscious holds the middle ground. The upper sextion (A) indicates the area belonging to consciousness, as seen in terms of psychic energy. The lower portion of the figure (B) indicates the area out of which unconscious reactions emerge which can "correct" consciousness. In the middle ground (C) the personal unconscious rests. This is the part of the unconscious that can be made conscious by the development of consciousness within the individual.

exaggerated activity, incomprehensible and inexplicable fears, depression and other similar phenomena.[8] The energy which is withdrawn from consciousness gives a greater intensity to unconscious contents, through which these contents intrude upon consciousness and cause disturbances. Keep in mind that symptoms and disturbances are also mechanisms to balance the psyche, and that the flowing of psychic energy does this. Psychic energy follows its own natural course here; flowing to a deficiency which needs to be filled. In terms of physics, this flow would only come to a standstill when there is equal energy everywhere and the deficiency is made good. Psychologically, however, the possibility exists of

[8]*Ibid*, p. 183.

channeling or partly turning aside the current through intervention from our consciousness. The creative power of the psyche lies in this: blind processes of nature don't always have to be blindly followed.

In regard to energy, the total psyche is seen as a closed system, in which the conscious and the unconscious interact with each other. The *personal* unconscious is considered part of the conscious system as far as energy is concerned, because its contents are psychologically connected with the ego or the *I* and therefore can be taken up into consciousness.[9] Figure 2.1. will illustrate this concept.

During the formation of the personality in childhood, for instance, a great deal of psychic energy is directed toward composing the ego. The child acts entirely in and from the unconscious, primarily from the collective unconscious. Since the child has had little time to gather and forget experience, the personal unconscious is still very small. The conscious and unconscious systems are hardly divided in a young child. At a given moment, the natural flow of psychic energy is subjected to a certain inexplicable interference whereby it begins to form an ego or *I*. A distinction begins to appear between the conscious and the unconscious parts of the psyche; consciousness then differentiates itself more and more in terms of functions and becomes a relatively closed system. The part of the psyche adjacent to the deeper levels of our unconscious becomes largely separated as a more conscious attitude is assumed. Differences in energy between the conscious and the unconscious system give rise to inner conflicts that express themselves in various ways at each age.

The young child shows a definite ambiguity: should he follow his own natural impulses, so strongly active in him, or should he adapt socially so that his ever-forming conscious self receives praise? In the adolescent, the disparity in energy expresses itself in the so-called *Sturm und Drang* period,[10] while the more mature individual experiences tension as he lives through inner pairs of contrasts (or, better, complementary functions) which demand a solution. Gradually these contrasts in consciousness decrease and a connection

[9]*Ibid*, p. 189.

[10]A term denoting the restlessness of adolescence and the insecurity felt during that period. It's a time for proving yourself a real "man" or "woman."

between consciousness and the unconscious can be established. This connection can be positive or negative; it can be maintained either through a stable but rigid attitude of consciousness, where changes are no longer allowed, or it can be maintained through the creation of a dynamic balance, where consciousness still adapts to change without so quickly losing its inner balance.

The connection between consciousness and the unconscious is established by the inferior function, or, astrologically speaking, by the inferior element, whose undeveloped condition draws energy to itself. The gradual adaptive attempts of the inferior element result more in the development of the entire personality than in a differentiation of consciousness. In regard to this point, Toni Wolff says, "...the firmly anchored consciousness becomes a function of the unlocked conscious awareness."[11] Psychic energy is sometimes called life energy because the flowing of energy always means that the psyche remains dynamic. This energy includes adaptation to both the outside world and its own inner world—the unconscious. The direction followed by psychic energy within the individual is closely connected with the astrological crosses, which I dealt with in *Astro-Psychology*. Before we go into specific astrological effects, it is necessary to look closer at the directions of the movement of psychic energy.

2. THE PROGRESSIVE AND REGRESSIVE DIRECTION OF ENERGY[12]

Our life is a process of continual adaptation. We are constantly dealing with both external circumstances that we cannot deny and with internal, often unconscious, factors that likewise cannot be ignored. We can speak of a continuing duality in our consciousness: every day we encounter something new in life which demands a decision based on a conscious or sometimes completely unconscious choice. Our path in life is a reflection of all of our choices. When we

---

[11]*Ibid*, p. 191.

[12]In this section, the following books have been used as reference: Wolff, T., *Studien zu C.G. Jungs Psychologie*, Teil III: Der Psychologische Energiebegriff, Rhein Verlag, Zurich, 1959, pp. 172-213; and Jung, C.G., *The Structure and Dynamics of the Psyche*, Collected Works, Vol 8, Routledge & Kegan Paul, London, 1977, pp. 3-67.

try to imagine what goes on in each person's consciousness it could be pictured as a "battle" taking place between two differing factions. Two extreme possibilities of choice (conscious or not) are asking for a decision. Once the choice has been made, the contents of "yes" remain important for our consciousness, while the contents of "no" disappear to the unconscious to join the countless other contents hidden there.

There are two ways we can adapt ourselves and influence our process of choice. The first way is to adapt ourselves as much as possible to the conscious demands of life, meeting the demands of the surroundings. When our psychic energy works this way, we speak of a *progressive direction*.[13] The progressive direction requires directedness of consciousness and attitude, but includes the risk of one-sidedness. It can easily happen that a particular attitude no longer provides the adaptation required by the surroundings, because changes in these surroundings demand another attitude.

For example, someone who naturally displays an attitude of feeling in his adaptation to the demands of reality may find himself in a situation that can only be resolved through thinking. In that case, the feeling response collapses and the progression of psychic energy (also called life energy or libido) also stops. The outward process of adaptation goes on strike! Psychic energy must then redirect itself and the goal becomes adaptation to inner needs. This is the second direction of psychic energy, the inward direction, or *regressive direction*.[14]

The progressive direction of the libido means that our superior function gradually beomes further developed and differentiated. This function, dealt with at length in the last chapter, determines the way in which we approach the world about us and therefore it deals with things outside ourselves. In the example just given, we can assume water formed the superior element and air the inferior. When insuffient energy is retained in consciousness, (in this case the element water), the process of regression automatically sets in.

[13]This is a psychological term and does not refer to astrological progressions or directions.

[14]Regressive direction is a psychological term, not to be confused with astrological *directions*.

The energy flows back into the unconscious and activates the inferior function there.

One thing should be remembered: the progressive movement is always characterized by the leading role played by the conscious system, whereby the inferior function, with its slight change, supplies just enough tension to accentuate the superior function until too much is repressed or one's approach becomes inadequate. Because the course of the energy can no longer aid the development of the superior function, congestion takes place. This congestion is accompanied by an intensification of the background contents of the psyche and by a continuing inadequacy of conscious adaptation. A fall appears between the conscious and unconscious systems whereby energy begins to flow back toward the unconscious— regression. The stronger the progression, the longer it lasts and the stronger the emphasis on outward adaptation. The more powerful then will be the regression, which is directed at adapting to the "forgotten" demands of the inner self. In *outward* adaptation (progression), subjective factors are all too often dismissed, since in such an adaptation there is always compromise with the divergent contents of one's own self. In regression, all these subjective factors come to the surface.

In contrast to the conscious directedness of the progressive movement, regression is not consciously directed, but is the natural course of psychic energy caused by the development of a "fall" or differences in charge. Therefore, regression is much less concerned with the superior function of consciousness than with the inferior element and its demands. In the first chapter, we learned that the inferior function is directly contrary to the superior conscious function, and because of the nature of this relationship, the inferior function often contains very "disturbing" contents for our conscious adaptation. Perhaps this is one of the reasons why so many people don't appreciate the regressive movement of psychic energy as much as the seemingly pleasant progressive movement. Yet we need both movements equally if we are to grow into integrated human beings.

For example, when fire is the superior function, earth will be the inferior. Earth has many characteristics that disturb fire. Earth loves security, fire adores the insecurity of future possibilities. Earth likes the here and now because it is sure. Fire always wants something new, thinking about what is ahead. If fire is superior, earth will be in the unconscious. When a breakthrough from the unconscious allows earth contents to intrude into consciousness, these contents hinder fire's free expression. Suddenly, the fire types may become very insecure, looking to enhance personal security. These are the people who suddenly want to find out where to obtain the highest interest on their savings, only to forget about the whole idea a few days later. A sudden wish from the unconscious took over the normal pattern. One fire type said to me, "I want to be more free than I am, so I think I will only work part time and I will have more time to do what I like." But his inferior element added, "But first I want to have at least $30,000 so that I won't have to worry about being poor." Obviously the earth contents have intruded on the fire, and the compulsion caused by the earth element has caused this person to continue working full time. This type of energy can be temporary, or in horoscopes with difficult divisions, the energy can last longer.

Carl Jung tried to explain the direction of psychic energy more clearly using the example of a river that flows from a mountain to a valley. Everything flows smoothly until it meets an obstruction, for instance, a dam blocks its course to the valley. If the obstruction is high enough, the water can be dammed up behind the barrier until the water level is high enough to continue flowing. This can occur in different ways. For instance, the current can follow its course in its own natural bed, or the water can be led into a channel, in which electrical energy is produced through means of a paddle wheel generator. In any case, the water flows outwards again, in the direction of the valley.

In terms of psychic energy, this can be expressed as follows: the river originally had a progressive direction, toward the outside world. Confronted with the dam, the river was forced to eddy in circles for a time, an action contrary to the prior direction of current. This eddying can be compared to the regressive movement. Once this has gone on long enough (the water level has become high enough), the progressive direction can be resumed. Sometimes it is even possible to make use of the apparent and temporary standstill (the damming of the water) to produce new energy (electricity can be generated, for instance), though this doesn't necessarily have to happen.

In the theory of psychic energy, progression is a means to come to regression, while, conversely, regression is a means to return to progression. Therefore, adaptation to the outer world (progression) eventually results in clearer perception of the needs of the inner world, because adaptation to this inner world becomes increasingly necessary (regression). Regression brings us more into balance, so we can readapt more effectively to the demands of our surroundings (progression). We can go along with one of these directions of current for a shorter or longer period, but it is the rhythmical alternation between both energy directions that gives us "vitality."

We shouldn't confuse progression with development, since an uninterrupted flow of life doesn't always include development and differentiation. Many forms of animal and plant life have existed from ancient times without further differentiation. In the same way, the psychic life of man can be progressive without there being any evolution to speak of, just as his psychic life can be regressive without showing involution.

Just as progression isn't synonymous with development, regression isn't necessarily a step backwards, although it can be at times. This doesn't necessarily imply degeneration. More often it is just one step in a total process of development, even though the individual may not be aware that he is undergoing any such development. Perhaps he feels himself to be caught in a compulsive situation, a situation corresponding in some ways to childhood. (The inferior function has been activated, after all!) Regression becomes degeneration if the individual tries to hold onto this condition and to identify with the unconscious contents that have emerged.

We should not confuse progression and regression with the terms *extroversion* and *introversion*. Extroversion and introversion can be both progressive and regressive. In other words, someone with a rather stable psychological attitude, who is also extroverted (oriented to the outer world) can be busy for a long time adapting to his own inner world, while outwardly showing little of this process. His attitude can thus remain extroverted, although his psychic energy is completely directed towards his unconscious.

3. The Three Crosses

In my book *Astro-Psychology*, I described the connection between the three crosses in astrology and the direction of psychic energy current or libido.[15] In this section, we will work out this theoretical background in practice.

If the examples that follow sometimes seem extreme or black and white, this is done as a means of putting the essential points into clear perspective. In practice, there are many different factors in a horoscope that can weaken or strengthen the total picture. To judge more fully, we must continually take the whole framework of the cross division into consideration. We will deal with this framework in the following section.

THE CARDINAL CROSS

In traditional astrology, *the cardinal cross* (Aries, Cancer, Libra and Capricorn) is attributed an outward orientation. Values are derived from the surroundings and adaptation to external circumstances plays a main role. Each of the four signs adapts in a completely unique way, corresponding to the four elements.

The outgoing, driving force corresponds to the previously described *progressive* direction of psychic energy. The process of adaptation to external circumstances is central to that direction as well. This doesn't mean that regression never occurs within these four signs. On the contrary, every person goes through progressive and regressive periods in the course of his life. However, the similarity between the cardinal signs and progressive energy lies in a primary focus on the outer world, without needing to make the division into extroversion or introversion. For cardinal people, adaptation to the demands of the outer world will continually take precedence over adaptation to the inner world.

For Aries, this implies a very impetuous attitude, including a desire to conquer, absorb, and fit everything into the mainstream of human experience. At first glance, this hardly resembles adaptation, since Aries sees everything from his own vantage point. However, adaptation to external circumstances in the sense of progressive energy doesn't necessarily imply a flexible social attitude. It is very possible to conform to outward matters and situations, adapting one's psychic direction to the external world, without becoming a

[15] Hamaker-Zondag, K.M., *Astro-Psychology,* Ch. 3.

socially adapted individual! The Aries individual is mainly directed to things outside himself, with which he can occupy himself and towards which he can direct his psychic energy. The situations Aries encounters can make him or break him.

The Cancer individual also conforms to outer norms; it is important for this water sign to know what people think so that he can act accordingly, and his own feelings are quickly adjusted to what is proper. This is a completely different way of expressing progressive energy than we saw with Aries. However, both signs direct energy outwards, just as do Libra and Capricorn.

Libra, like Cancer, derives its values from the surroundings, but being specifically oriented towards social intercourse, it also participates in forming these social values. Flexibility, harmony and balance in relationships are central for this sign, so that here we also see adaptation to the demands of the surroundings, although in a rather mental way.

Capricorn derives its values from the surroundings very concretely. He therefore prefers to undertake purposeful, practical, and preferably prominent work, whereby he attempts to lead everything into channels according to fixed patterns. Capricorn is a maker of laws and regulations, to which he also submits himself. This sign, despite an often quiet, introverted manner, is also strongly involved in what happens around it, and adapts in its own earth sign way.

The cardinal cross, which represents progressive energy, very definitely needs exchange and cooperation with its surroundings, no matter how this is expressed. The signs Aries and Capricorn relate most things directly to themselves; the signs Cancer and Libra relate a great deal to other people as well, which indirectly reflects back upon themselves.

THE FIXED CROSS

The *fixed cross* (Taurus, Leo, Scorpio, and Aquarius) most closely corresponds with regressive energy. Again, this doesn't mean that people with fixed signs strong in their horoscopes constantly live in a regressive manner; rather, they are mainly directed toward adapting to the inner self and inner felt values. In complete correspondence with the laws of the psyche, they will normally experience periods of progression as well. Their main unconscious concern is to straighten out their own unconscious contents, no matter what the world may think. Naturally, this doesn't always happen without crises. This cross is not called the Cross of Christ or the cross of crisis for nothing.

Having an adaptation process predominantly directed to the demands of the unconscious, these fixed signs will be confronted with their own unconscious, in which the inferior element plays the main role. Directly contrary to our conscious attitude, it is the least developed element and largely uncontrolled in its activity. Since the psychic energy of the fixed signs is primarily directed toward unfolding and exploring the unconscious, conscious energy is invested in the inferior element. Therefore, it can make itself strongly felt. Moreover, a fixed sign has an absolute need to continually bring to the surface that which is contrary to its conscious self, in order to realize an inner balance, often a lengthy and difficult process. As the inferior element becomes more important, the characteristics belonging to that element seem to form part of the conscious element. The following section will clarify the intense inner polarity in reference to the four signs themselves.

A Taurus can stay with something for an extremely long time and deal with it very conscientiously. Even though a business has long been declared a lost cause, Taurus will still work faithfully for it, because he still sees something in it. "To see perspective in something" is a typical characteristic of fire, the inferior element for Taurus. Being directed toward inner adaptation, he will take fire characteristics into his conscious attitude, but they still retain their inferior character. Consciously he can't work with them, yet they play an important role for him. They may even be the source of his feeling of loyalty. In practice, this can have both positive and negative results. On one hand, he runs the risk of wasting his energy on lost causes, stubbornly staying too long. On the other hand, Taurus can help an organization or group through a difficult period by continuing to work as though nothing were wrong. His daily life is therefore a combination of a superior earth element (sensation) and an inferior fire element (intuition) which his regressive tendency regularly brings to the surface.

Leo, a fire sign, shows the reverse picture. Parts of the unconscious inferior earth element are often revealed in the Leo attitude. Leo's need for luxury, mentioned in every classical astrology text, can be seen as an expression of this earth element coming to the surface. Of its own accord, a fire sign doesn't care much about material things—the concrete or material is their weakest point. Yet, for a fire sign, Leo is very attached to the material and concrete: the element earth in his unconscious, activated through his regressive tendency, is playing a role in his consciousness. The inferior function often forms that part of our psyche that we try to silence through overcompensation because it creates uncertainty. Leo's sometimes exaggerated display of luxury and material beauty can easily express uncertainty about the material world. Through his material emphasis, he can derive a certain feeling of security.

Scorpio also digs into the unconscious—and in fact is known for this. This water sign, experienced by the world as very emotional, is nonetheless constantly ordering and analyzing everything it experiences. This is a typical air characteristic, but air is the inferior element for a water sign. Here again, the unconscious function is re-activated by the predominantly regressive energy of the fixed sign. Scorpio's digging into the unconscious is thus a combination of a feeling evaluation and an experiencing of events, on the one hand, and a constant endeavor to analyze and explain things mentally, on the other. In accordance with the compulsive nature of the inferior function, Scorpio's analytic approach sometimes seems to predominate—at least to the outside world.

The last fixed sign, Aquarius, is generally known as having a people-oriented approach and a need to exchange ideas and thoughts. Yet this is only an apparent adaptation to the outer world in that he is interested in the world but he holds on as long as possible to his own world view and framework of ideas, and his view is largely derived from his own inner self. Aquarius adheres longest to theories or images of the world which have an emotional value for him; in other words, to those things which connect him with his inferior unconscious water element. Anyone who has thoroughly studied the signs has probably noticed how much Aquarius becomes involved in emotional situations and, more than any other sign, holds on (consciously) or remains attached (unconsciously) to them. Although as an air sign Aquarius will naturally try to rationalize everything, often things only have meaning when they touch his feelings and therefore release something in him that he *can't* rationalize. With his tendency to direct energy mainly towards his own inner self, he won't pass up any chance to experience something completely. He is searching for the essence of all things, in an attempt to fit everything into his mental picture of the world. Aquarius' talent for psychology derives largely from this combination of superior thinking (air) and unconcious inferior feeling (water).

THE MUTABLE CROSS

The third cross in astrology, containing the mutable signs Gemini, Virgo, Sagittarius and Pisces, doesn't always show itself clearly. Some astrologers find it weak in its manner of expression.[16] Others find it a synthesis of the preceding two crosses, while still others call this cross pre-eminently changeable, flexible and accommodating.[17]

Psychologically, the mutable cross has no fixed direction for its energy: it is neither regressive nor progressive, and can express itself in both forms. The mutable cross temporarily follows a regressive or progressive direction in turn, yet neither direction is predominant. Therefore, this cross plays a unique role in the psyche, which we can best illustrate once more by Carl Jung's example of the river. The progressive direction corresponds with the natural downward flow of the river from the mountain to the valley, while the regressive energy direction corresponds with the temporary effect of the water being dammed by a barrier in the river. Once the lake that is formed has collected enough water, the water can be led away (for instance, in a canal), so that the progressive direction again prevails. The mutable cross plays a dual role in this process: on one hand, this cross is able to turn progressive energy into regressive energy through laying a dam, and, on the other hand, the mutable cross is able to release the dammed up energy by forming a channel so progression can start again.

[16]Kündig, H., *Das Horoskop*, Die Berechnung, Darstellung und Erklärung. Ansata Verlag, Zürich, 1950, pp. 171-172.

[17]For various approaches to the crosses see: Jansky, R.C., *Selected Topics in Astrology*, Van Nuys, Ca., 1974, p. 28; Hone, M.E., *The Modern Textbook of Astrology*, Fowler, London, 1970, p. 42; Libra, C. Aq., *Astrologie, haar Techniek Ken Ethiek*, Amersfoort, 1923, p. 42; Arroyo, S., *Astrology, Psychology, and the Four Elements*, CRCS, Reno, 1975, pp. 87-170.

This dualistic function is one possible explanation for the outwardly elusive quality of the mutable. On one hand, the mutable cross can work in an extremely stimulating and adaptable way, and on the other, it is just as capable of bringing in all sorts of obstructions, and thus achieving the opposite. We will constantly find this mutable cross on the junction or turning-point of psychic energy, as in figure 2.2.

Mutable energy is always revolving in the transition from the conscious to the unconscious, being alternately active in one or the other. In certain respects, mutable energy is a synthesis of the progressive and regressive direction, as it includes both. The very fact that the energy keeps revolving around the middle allows the possibility of maintaining both the progressive and regressive directions of energy in balance.

This is probably why wisdom and harmony were traditionally attributed to this cross, although this concept does not mean people born in mutable signs are paragons of wisdom. Rather, the mutable cross is a means for the psyche to dissolve, integrate, and change so

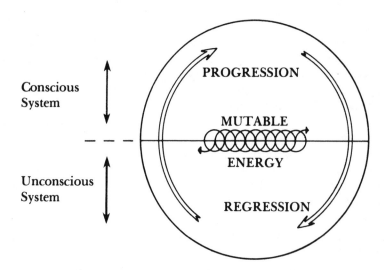

Figure 2.2. The mutable cross illustrates the constant interplay of action between the conscious and unconscious facets of the expression of the energy of the psyche.

that part of the ego disappears or loses some of its value for the whole psyche; only then can one experience things as they really are, without the self being in the way. That *can* lead to wisdom and harmony, but it also includes the danger of becoming estranged from oneself, due to preoccupation with this middle area of the psyche. Once a mutable type has landed in this no man's land, only through contact with strongly progressive or regressive types will he be able to re-experience the depths of his own personality. Otherwise, he must find a way to activate his own regressive and progressive possibilities. The mutable cross, therefore, symbolizes a transition between the progressive and the regressive psychic energy, while at the same time it includes both. This is an apparent duality that is expressed in the dualistic character of the mutable signs as well.

Of the two means of expression for the mutable cross, namely setting up a psychic obstruction (creating a dam) or setting the psychic progression in motion once more (laying a drainage canal), the latter is most apparent. Energy flows outward and is more directly experienced by the person himself and his surroundings. The formation of a dam in the psychic energy current, however, is equally a feature of the mutable cross. The goal is to correct excessive actions of the psyche by reversing the direction of psychic energy and bringing about harmony or balance once more. The formation of a dam, in order that the lake may fill up, also means simultaneously that this same mutable energy will begin forming the new drainage canal. (In extreme cases, the water will never reach any significant level.) This mechanism also characterizes the outward service orientation of the mutable type, as the function of serving corresponds with the meaning of service traditionally attributed to this cross.

This attitude of service is also expressed in another area. When a horoscope is either markedly progressive (cardinal) or regressive (fixed), the mutable cross will be subordinate to the main tendency up to a certain point, while continuing to express unmistakably an essential part of its mutable character. In such a case, we can see a great degree of compliance with the other directions of energy, while the mutable cross retains its own transitional function. For example, a Sagittarius (mutable) may have most of his planets, and even the Ascendant, in fixed signs, and may therefore look rather fixed and oriented toward inner adaptation. When you observe this person closely, however, you may see that he is still mutable, expressing this energy in a subtle way, and he will be more flexible than may be apparent on first sight.

In contrast, a person having strong mutable signs and houses will show a different picture. Psychic energy continually circles around the transistion area between consciousness and the unconscious; the conscious system and the unconscious contents predominate in turn. It is difficult for this person or those around him to have a clear image of what he really is as a person. In many cases, self-evaluation doesn't interest him anyhow, unless other contents of his horoscope contradict. It isn't a question he worries about. Having both regressive and progressive directions, he can revert to extremes without wanting to become fixed in either extreme. In that sense, the mutable cross is then literally mutable.

The risk of becoming stuck is inherent in the mutability of this cross, something that is often ignored. This type takes life as it comes, so that adaptation within that narrow border of the psyche often appears more important than assimilation. There is danger that the mutable type will continue to build dams or drainage canals for himself and other people, without ever straightening out his own conscious or unconscious self. When the regressive current doesn't develop any further, the new progressive direction is not as intense as it would have been with a greater depth of regression. The stronger the regressive movement is within the psyche, the clearer the resulting progression will be. This is one possible explanation for Kündig's description of the mutable cross as having little intensity. With the very strong mutable types, this continual inner attempt to create balance can result in a lack of actual, outward balance. The person ignores actual problems or fools himself into thinking that the problem is solved almost as soon as it is recognized, when in reality one has just begun to tackle the problem.

On the other hand, the mutable signs can be very flexible in their approach to life, each in its own way, naturally. Being in a position of transition means that mutable signs can obstruct themselves considerably without noticing it (the dam under construction) but they can also make it easy for themselves by going on as usual despite all their problems (the canal under construction).

The fact that mutable energy has no clear direction, is active only in a limited area, and therefore is difficult to discern, may be one reason why this form of psychic energy is never really described as a separate case in analytical psychology. In the following material, the dangers that can arise from the duality of the mutable cross will receive some emphasis, since, in my opinion, very little has been said in astrology about this. This has nothing to do with a negative evaluation of the mutable signs. On the contrary, it is only for the sake of clarity that they are represented somewhat in caricature.

Gemini, the first mutable sign, is well known for his attitude of "trimming his sails to every wind." The amount of information this sign is able to collect and relate borders on the incredible. Yet he seldom builds a coherent view of the world; everything is left to the circumstances of the moment. Gemini is the happy-go-lucky merrymaker, but he lacks self-knowledge and this can estrange him strongly from himself. As overcompensation, Gemini can pry into the emotional life of others—the natural hunger for information remains—with the result that he can become quite shameless, becoming a walking gossip column filled with the latest news. This is exactly the opposite of the essentially cheerful, vivacious nature of Gemini who prefers to dig canals so that the water can flow again, yet the sign can become a dam for both himself and others.

Virgo, the second mutable sign, is known for its analytical ability which largely serves the idea that everything must be pure. Virgo is a pure sign, and for that reason chastity is usually connected astrologically with this sign. Virgo's constant dissection and consideration of things can result in a complete estrangement from himself: no connections are made, one's own self is looked at very critically and the whole disintegrates into small pieces. When there are no compensating tendencies in the horoscope, Virgo may change into the very opposite of its true nature through this mutable energy. It may seek the pure and pristine in what is not pure and pristine at all. Hence, chastity may lapse into bouts of excessive sexual activity, in the hope this immersion will provide a synthesis which cannot be arrived at through consciousness. The contrast between the inborn moderation of its own nature and the exuberant immoderation of the other side is both bridged and made sharper by Virgo's mutable energy. The mutability makes it possible to unite both sides in one person, but if this synthesis is ignored, it is still possible for Virgo to survive this duality without too much psychic damage. It may not even be much of a hindrance for Virgo.

Sagittarius, the third mutable sign, prefers to spread the information it has found and synthesized. Oriented toward teaching others and needing to investigate and judge everything, he is constantly examining everything around him. Yet he tends to overlook himself. In his mutable fire ardor to put all his discoveries into the right terms, comprehensible for everyone, he risks getting stuck in transmitting information, while his eyes and ears are closed to information that could revise these opinions. His message can then become superficial, rigid dogma, and his life an expression of that dogma, while the human being himself lacks expression. Mutability then appears to be stuck, and the individual may seem to be more obstinate than those born into the fixed signs. The willingness of the mutable cross to adapt is no longer evident. Sagittarius then seems to have become constricted in the opposite of his true nature, by the same energy that could help him to break through his rigidity.

Pisces, the last mutable sign, combines mutability with a feeling (water) approach. This element is still capable of recognizing certain realities, but the mutable cross makes sure that some "extras" are added to these values. Pisces easily fits everything into his feeling world, but the ease with which this occurs means that not everything is tested for value or for its degree of reality. Often the process of assimilation takes place only later. An increasing number of unreal factors can begin to form reality for Pisces and, finally, to predominate. Therefore the danger of coming to live in a self-created dream world is always present. No longer able to experience his own self as such in this dream world, he begins to play an imaginary role and can become estranged from himself. Because all energy is focused on creating ideals and dreams for a non-existent reality, his rich inner life is robbed of its creative power. Once more, it is the mutable energy which can help Pisces out of this situation or help him remain completely untroubled by it, even though those around him may think differently.

A definite directed movement was evident with progressive (cardinal) energy, and an undirected yet clearly distinguishable movement with regressive (fixed) energy. Mutable energy, however, only shows movement without any fixed direction. To say that mutable energy runs the risk of stagnating sounds paradoxical, yet it is not. In this case, the energy has retreated into a very narrow area on the borderline between consciousness and the unconscious. The drainage canal is being dug as soon as the dam begins to be constructed. The progressive and regressive fluctuation is minimal and mutability is nearly at a standstill. Life concentrates itself in a narrow, impersonal border area and can no longer identify with what is above or below. The resulting immovability and lack of flexibility have nothing in common with the tenacity attributed to the fixed cross. The fixed cross can ultimately arrive at a more flexible attitude because of a tenacious delving into its own unconscious. In this respect, the cardinal cross can be said to be somewhere between the mutable and the fixed cross. For instance, someone with a cardinal Sun and all other planets in fixed signs, will show strong regressive tendencies, despite his Sun sign's more progressive direction.

As mentioned earlier, in judging the direction of energy, it isn't correct to consider only the Sun sign, no matter how important the Sun might be in the horoscope. For a clear overall picture it is necessary to make a diagram of the crosses—something we will discuss in the following section.

4. How To Determine Cross Divisions

We first make a classification into potential and circumstances (that is, signs and houses) for the division of the crosses, just as we did with the element division of the horoscope. We check the cardinal cross planets first by listing all the planets found in Aries, Cancer, Libra and Capricorn. Next we look at the first, fourth, seventh, and tenth houses. The fixed cross includes Taurus, Leo, Scorpio and Aquarius, and the fixed houses are the second, fifth, eighth and eleventh. The mutable cross includes Gemini, Virgo, Sagittarius, and Pisces, along with the third, sixth, ninth and twelfth houses.

After each cross we note which planets are found there (in the sign column). Note the sign of the Ascendant and the Midheaven as well. We repeat this for the houses, so that we have a picture of how potential relates to experience and circumstances. As with the element division, we can sum up all the contents, but this total doesn't necessarily tell us anything about the real strength of the cross. Before we can make a judgement we must make a distinction

Crosses	Signs	Houses	Total
CARDINAL	♃ ♄ ⛢	☽ ♃ ♀ ♄ ⛢	8
FIXED	☿ ☉ ♂ ♇ Asc.	☿ ♄	7
MUTABLE	♀ Mc. ♄ ☽	☉ ♂ ♇	7

Figure 2.3. An illustration of the crosses as they appear in Fred's horoscope. See Chart 1 on page 14.

between personal and impersonal planets, as we did in the previous section.

We can make the same sort of list that we did in Chapter 1. The division of the crosses in Fred's horoscope (Chart 1 on page 14) is shown in figure 2.3. Figure 2.4 illustrates Marilyn Monroe's horoscope (see Chart 2 on page 18).

In figure 2.4. you will see that we have applied the rule that when a planet is located close to the cusp of the following house, it comes into expression in the following house (as discussed in Chapter 1, Section 3). In Marilyn's chart, Venus is located within four degrees of an angular house, near the Midheaven (or the cusp of the tenth house) and isn't retrograde. Venus remains in the sign of Aries, but in regard to houses Venus is counted as being in effect in the tenth house.

Crosses	Signs	Houses	Total
CARDINAL	♀ ♇	⛢ ♄ ☽ ♃ ♀	7
FIXED	Mc. Asc. ⛢ ♄ ☽ ♃	♂ ☿ ☉	9
MUTABLE	☉ ♀ ♂ ♄	♄ ♇	6

Figure 2.4. The cardinal, fixed and mutable planets and houses in Marilyn Monroe's chart. See Chart 2 on page 18. As you will notice, the planets are not entered in the order of the planetary motion in the zodiac, but as they appear in the chart.

5. Cross Division Interpretation

In the first part of one's life, potential (sign) plays a greater role than circumstance (house). Therefore we need to look first at the planets in the signs, and only then can we examine any shifts that might occur through the planet being located in a house belonging to another cross.

In Fred's chart (page 14), three of the most important personal contents, symbolized by Sun, Mercury, and the Ascendant, are located in fixed signs. In potential, therefore, one can speak of a regressive movement of energy, which demands that consciousness adapt to its own inner norms. The mutable signs contain some important personal contents as well: the Moon, Venus and Midheaven. Though this mutable energy can give support to the regressive movement in many respects, Fred will show fewer traits from the fixed cross and more progression (mutability) as he grows older. The fixed cross plays a much smaller role in his circumstances (houses) than it does in potential (sign), even though Mercury in Taurus repeats itself by being in a fixed house (the fifth). The Sun and Mars in fixed signs must express themselves in mutable houses, while the Moon and Venus, located in mutable signs, bring their mutable energy to bear on the cardinal houses that show a progressive movement of energy. (We are restricting ourselves to personal planets.) In all respects, Fred shows a gradual shift in his center of gravity: fixed to mutable, mutable to cardinal. This means that a more balanced division of energy can take place as Fred grows older, and also that the mutable cross, which necessarily marks the position of transition, will become increasingly important. The fixed sign ability to persevere, the driving force behind the will to experience and assimilate, is helped by the ability of the mutable cross energy to make things relative. Moreover, the increasing importance of the cardinal energy helps make the values of the surroundings seem less pressing at the same time that there is a growing willingness to meet certain outer demands halfway. One advantage of this division is that the division of psychic energy becomes relatively balanced. One disadvantage can be that, because of this relative balance, the need of the fixed cross to digest things and conform solely to itself no longer can be fulfilled. And despite a growing balance, he will occasionally feel unsatisfied, especially since this horoscope shows such a strong occupation of the fixed signs.

In Fred's case, the shifts can occur gradually, without too many shocks. By shifts, we mean the transfer of the way a planet (content) expresses itself (determined by the cross it's in) into circumstances (determined by another cross) as indicated by the house. A shift from fixed to cardinal or vice versa (regression and progression) can cause the greatest problems if the horoscope shows no support for the transition.

The second horoscope (Marilyn Monroe in Chart 2 on page 18) shows problematical shifts. The potential is mutable (Sun and Mercury) with a fixed undertone (Midheaven, Ascendant and the Moon). That fixed cross becomes increasingly important because the Sun and Mercury are in fixed houses, whil the mutable houses contain no personal planets. Many of the planets in fixed signs shift to cardinal houses, so tension arises between a regressive direction in fixed sign planets which must express themselves in progression. By itself, that wouldn't necessarily be serious; however, in this division, something personal is lacking in the transitional (mutable) cross, at least in house position. See figure 2.4. In potential, Marilyn was able to maintain a balance between progression and regression, though the relation between potential and circumstance threatened to become more strained as she grew older. Her ability to change to a regressive movement when problems appeared, as well as to withdraw from a regressive situation by finding new channels, had difficulty expressing itself through her life circumstances. Her planets in mutable signs found themselves moreover in fixed houses,

Crosses	Signs	Houses	Total
CARDINAL	☉ ♄ ♂ ♅	♃ ☽	6
FIXED	☽ Mc. ♇ Asc. ♀ ♃	♄ ♂ ☿ ☉ ♇	11
MUTABLE	♄ ☿	♅ ♀ ♇	5

Figure 2.5. The cardinal, fixed and mutable planets and houses in Peter's chart. See Chart 3 on page 42 in order to follow along with the entries made here.

except for Uranus. In contrast, her feminine contents, the Moon and Venus, expressed through cardinal houses. In fact, her cross division is very different than Fred's horoscope: there we saw an increasing balance, while, here, we see a growing duality. This second horoscope, therefore, offers the possibility of experiencing life very intensely, but it also includes the danger of extreme states of mind.

The third and last example, Peter's horoscope (Chart 3 on page 42), shows us a broad picture. The Sun is in a cardinal sign, the Moon, Midheaven and Ascendant are in fixed signs, and Mercury is in a mutable. With the distribution shown in figure 2.5, it is difficult to give a clear opinion about which cross is most decisive in sign. The Sun becomes more decisive in such a distribution, but at the same time more vulnerable. Within this cross division, the cardinal cross comes first, with some reservations, which means that the progressive energy direction is important, although the houses also help determine that this direction is maintained.

The Moon presented as fixed in potential (sign), actually appears in a cardinal house, but the most striking thing is the strong shift of planets from cardinal and mutable signs to fixed houses. In many cases, this would be an indication that despite the initial progressive movement, regression will play an increasingly important role, especially since the mutable Mercury must be active in a fixed house. By such a broad sign distribution, the houses become decisive in meaning at a much earlier age. In Peter's horoscope, we can already see during his first Moon-Saturn cycle,[18] an increasing tendency to measure himself by his own values, even though, as an Aries, he is strongly oriented to the outer world.

Up to a certain point, Venus in a mutable house (the sixth) gives the possibility of forming a bridge between one energy direction and another, because Venus belongs to the personal planets. Characteristically, Peter feels most at ease and in harmony with himself when he activates his own Venus, both in love relationships with women and in his artistic occupations: he is a musician. (Such a personal planet in a bridging position was completely lacking in Marilyn Monroe's horoscope. In her case, only the eruptive planets, Uranus and Pluto, were located in

---

[18]For a complete discussion of Moon-Saturn cycle, please see my book *Astro-Psychology*.

mutable houses, which offers hardly any hold for conscious experience and assimilation of circumstances.)

The crosses really only take on meaning when we connect them with the elements of the horoscope, while the element division gains new dimension through the crosses. The interpretation of only a single element or only one cross remains extremely limited. The combination of both of these basic factors in the horoscope will serve as a general frame of reference to analyze the horoscope further. In the following chapter, we will combine elements and crosses.

CHAPTER THREE

ELEMENTS AND CROSSES:
FOUNDATION FOR STRUCTURE OF PERSONALITY

1. THE DIFFERENCE BETWEEN ELEMENT AND CROSS

Before we discuss the combined effect of the elements and the crosses, it may be useful to note once more the difference between these two astrological concepts. The elements indicate the way one views and experiences the world, whereby we can distinguish four basic possibilities: thinking (air), feeling (water), intuition (fire) and sensation (earth). *One* of these functions predominates in consciousness, becoming the superior function, which determines the attitude of consciousness. The inferior function is located in the unconscious, opposite the main function of consciousness. The two remaining functions or elements can develop into auxiliary functions of consciousness.

Therefore, the element primarily says something about a person's view of the world, the attitude of consciousness, and the way he experiences and judges everything he meets. These ways of experiencing and these attitudes of consciousness still do not tell us how someone *adapts* to events and circumstances, nor about the processes of assimilation and adaptation. The crosses provide information about these psychic processes while the elements give us information about the contents of the horoscope. They show the basis upon which a person constructs his world view and the element from which one might expect counteractions to come. The crosses, on the other hand, give us *no* information about contents, but rather information about the *processes* which regulate both the relation between the elements themselves and between the person and his environment.

Combining the four elements with the three crosses is bound to fail if we are unable to distinguish the crosses from the specific attitudes of consciousness which we have attributed to the elements. We can best illustrate this elementary difference with an example. When four different elements look at a white tea cup, the earth element will perceive it concretely: it is white, it has a handle and a specific form. The air element is able to distinguish it as a tea cup and allots it a place in the series of phenomena air encounters. Water feels whether it finds the tea cup beautiful and whether it is pleasant to drink from, and on the basis of this, water gives the cup a certain value. The fire element, on the other hand, has had its imagination set loose by seeing the cup, and perceives all the things one might do with the cup. Fire sees the invisible connection, as it were, between the cup and everything else that can be related to it.

When the element earth, on the basis of its concrete, sensory perception, says it is a beautiful cup, earth is saying that the cup's proportion, color, and other external factors are pleasing. When the fire element agrees that the cup is beautiful, on the other hand, it is speaking from an entirely different world. Very possibly the fire type can't even describe what the cup looks like and finds it beautiful because of the unconscious stimulation fire receives when all the possibilities of the cup come to him. This can lead to misunderstanding; both elements speak their own language from their own world and often don't understand that other worlds exist, or at least can't identify with the other element's way of experiencing things. Enormous confusion in language can occur on account of the elements' differences in perspective, even though they use the same words.

Such verbal confusions may also take place within the inner self of every individual; consciousness and the unconscious are compensating each other through all sorts of actions and counteractions. The elements which diametrically diagree with each other are fire-earth and air-water. When a verbal misunderstanding occurs between the superior and the inferior element, some mediation must take place. The psychic energy current makes this connection, which is symbolized astrologically by the crosses. For an understanding of how this can happen, Jung describes the behavior of psychic energy in relation to the four functions of consciousness as a process of adaptation that requires a directed conscious function. This function would be characterized by an inner consistency and some logical coherence. Astrologically this is the element. Because the process of adaptation is directed, everything unsuitable must be excluded in order to maintain the integrity of direction. Jung says that unsuitable elements are inhibited and may escape attention. There is only *one* consciously directed function of adaptation and this astrologically is the superior element. If someone has a thinking orientation that person can't orient himself by feeling, because thinking and feeling are two different functions. Feeling would have to be excluded if the logical laws of thinking are to be satisfied as thought-process cannot be disturbed by the feeling function. In this case libido is withdrawn from the feeling process, and this function becomes relatively unconscious. The inferior functions are activated by regression and when they reach consciousness, they may appear in some incompatible form that is disguised and covered up with the slime of the deep. The stoppage of libido (psychic energy) may be due to a failure of the conscious attitude, and valuable seeds lie in the unconscious contents waiting to be activated by regression. They include elements of functions excluded by the conscious attitude.[1]

A number of important points emerge from this. We see that the verbal confusion between the conscious attitude and unconscious contents can be resolved through the current of psychic energy. Psychic energy (derived from the astrological crosses) connects the four elements in the psyche. The crosses themselves are not connected with the contents of the unconscious or the conscious self, but the results of the current of psychic energy *can* bring about changes in the contents of both areas of the psyche.

We can consider the flowing of psychic energy as a means to straighten out both ourselves and our relation to the world. After a process of assimilation and settling (the regression), progression will start once more: adaptation to the outside world. In the complete process of progression and regression, mutable energy marks both transitional positions.

---

[1] Jung, Carl, G., On Psychic Energy, *The Structure and Dynamics of the Psyche*, Collected Works Vol. 8., Routledge & Kegan Paul, London, 1977, pp. 35-36.

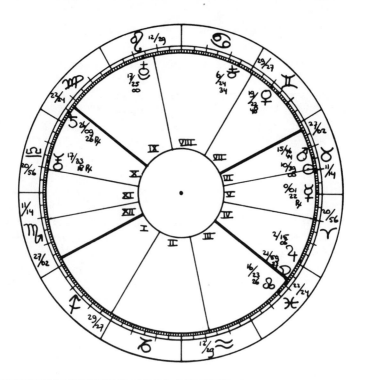

Elements	Signs	Houses	Total
FIRE	♃ ♇	♇ ☿	4
EARTH	☿ ☉ ♂ ♄ Mc.	☉ ♂ ♄ ♇	9
AIR	♀ ♇	♀	3
WATER	♅ Asc. ☽	☽ ♃ ♇	6

Crosses	Signs	Houses	Total
CARDINAL	♃ ♇ ♅	☽ ♃ ♀ ♄ ♇	8
FIXED	☿ ☉ ♂ ♇ Asc.	☿ ♅	7
MUTABLE	♀ Mc. ♄ ☽	☉ ♂ ♇	7

2. ELEMENTS AND CROSSES INTERPRETED TOGETHER

Now that we understand that the astrological elements represent our psychological view of the world and the astrological crosses symbolize the way we assimilate all these impressions, we can consider Chart 1 again. The arrangement of the elements were discussed in Chapter 1 and the arrangement of the crosses in Chapter 2. Consequently, we can now consider how both factors can be brought into synthesis. Fred's chart and the breakdown of his elements and crosses are presented again in figure 3.1.

Fred's superior function is earth, which means that his way of viewing, evaluating, and experiencing everything around him is practical, concrete, and factual. Because of a strong fixed cross by sign, the assimilation process will be slow-working and profound, whether he wants it to be or not. The emphasis on the fixed cross will bring to the surface of the psyche his inferior element of fire, and secondly the element air, so that the planets in those elements will play a strong, if archaic, role for his consciousness. During the first half of his life he may have difficulty with this. Confronted with his inferior element and being afflicted with such a slow-working process of assimilation in potential (the fixed signs), he will plunge into his own depths time and time again. There is no law that says he will be bothered by this, but it may cause feelings of insecurity. These feeling can propel him in two directions: he may cling to what security he does have (in agreement with his Sun in Taurus), or, if his inferior fire element comes to the surface, he may start looking more for possibilities and solutions.

In the first half of our lives, in many cases, we are still busy experiencing all the extremes in ourselves; afterwards, we tend to level off and prefer the middle road. Therefore, Fred will probably feel both tendencies in himself in the first half of his life: clinging to certainties as well as searching intensely for possibilities to experience. The certainties will predominate because of their relation with the conscious superior function. As he grows older, mutable energy will become more important, indicating a growing need to make things relative. This is accompanied by the cardinal cross becoming more important, so assimilation gradually becomes

Figure 3.1. Fred's chart. For this discussion, the element and cross totals are also included.

less regressive, and Fred will also begin to pay more attention to his surroundings. He will become increasingly aware of the demands of his surroundings and will satisfy these demands to some degree, although the potential always remains stronger. He will continue to conform primarily to his own inner values, although they become less compulsive. This is both a positive and a negative development, as I indicated in the chapter on the crosses, depending upon how we see it. In any case, Fred will become more open to the world, but his potential to adapt to his own self is so strong that inner conflicts arise. The elements of fire and air will play an important role in any inner conflict, both as factors to cause disturbances and as factors to smooth things out.

When we diagnose the basic construction of the horoscope, the tensions, inhibitions, and possibilities of the psyche will emerge clearly. When you see strong elementary tension in the horoscope (for instance, when such polar elements as air and water are each strongly occupied), that tension will play a decisive role in the, character. Yet we must never conclude that this causes a person to be terribly unhappy. Elementary tension has nothing to do with whether a person feels contented or unhappy, but indicates how consciousness orients itself, how experiences will be assimilated, and where we can expect compensating reactions to originate. Such counteractions can contain both painful and pleasurable experiences.

Much depends upon our attitude towards our total psyche. For instance, a horoscope with air strongly occupied but with the Moon in a water sign, can actually enjoy a supersentimental or melancholy mood now and then. The person doesn't necessarily experience any pain because of this, even though the Moon is active from the unconscious inferior function. On the contrary, experiencing such moods through the Moon in a water sign can even help maintain inner balance, although the Moon's location in the inferior element strengthens this element tension. Tension can work in a very creative way and has nothing to do, I repeat, with whether or not one feels good. These feelings are primarily indicated by the location of the planets and their relationships with each other.

Therefore, the strong tension shown in Chart 2 doesn't mean that Marilyn Monroe felt very unhappy, although her element tension gave a sort of hungry feeling that is difficult to put into words. It comes down to a dissatisfaction with things as they are, arising from a vague awareness that there must be *more*, and that there is still so much that is unfulfilled, though one rarely knows *what*. For convenience, see figure 3.2 on page 80, as we have combined Chart 2 and figure 1.3 from Chapter 1 with figure 2.4 from Chapter 2 so the reader can follow the discussion easily.

The distribution in Marilyn's horoscope indicates a great deal of tension in potential, both in regard to the crosses and the elements. This element tension gave her the unsatisfied feeling we mentioned, which she could experience as unpleasant; but this same tension gave her something very stimulating—the driving force behind her desire for still more. The strong duality between the superior air element, through which she logically experienced and approached the world, and the inferior water element—occupied by impersonal planets—would be obvious to both herself and her surroundings.

The strong occupation of the fixed and mutable crosses indicates that the inner self (her unconscious) would make its demands. The fixed cross means one continually tries to adapt to inner demands—to that which is inexplicable and irrational—for these demands emerge from the unconscious and press on one's consciousness. Since the fixed and mutable crosses were equal in potential, the compulsion to adapt to her own inner self would be eased because the mutable cross offered the possibility of withdrawing into herself and reappearing when it was necessary. The mutable cross barely appears in circumstances (house position), indicating a danger that she could be less flexible about changing from one inner situation to another than her potential promised. The cardinal houses, in contrast, receive more emphasis, which means that once she was headed in a certain psychic direction, she could stay put longer. The fixed houses also receive a strong emphasis. All of this together means that her mutability lost importance as she grew older and as experience began to play a greater role in her life. At the same time, the growing emphasis on the cardinal and fixed houses means that the psychic energy, which maintains contact between consciousness and the unconscious, became just as dualistic as the division of the elements indicates. A strong emphasis on cardinality gives a strong need to satisfy the demands of the outside world, whereas a strong fixed cross gives priority to the needs of one's own inner world. In her case, consciousness and the unconscious were sharply opposite each

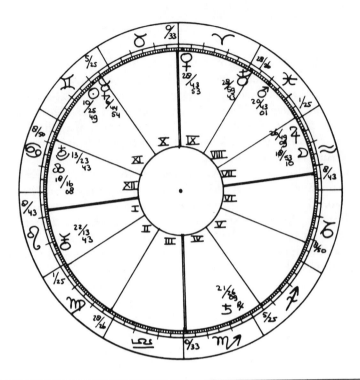

Elements	Signs	Houses	Total
FIRE	♀ Asc. ⛢	⛢ ♄	5
EARTH	Mc.	♀	2
AIR	☿ ☉ ☽ ♃	☉ ☿ ♃ ☽	8
WATER	♇ ♄ ♂ ⛢	♄ ♂ ♇	7

Crosses	Signs	Houses	Total
CARDINAL	♀ ♇	⛢ ♄ ☽ ♃ ♀	7
FIXED	Mc. Asc. ⛢ ♄ ☽ ♃	♂ ☿ ☉	9
MUTABLE	☉ ☿ ♂ ⛢	⛢ ♇	6

other. Psychic energy, symbolized by the crosses, strengthened her conscious air attitude through the cardinal cross, while an equally strong fixed cross (already strong in sign) gave the opposite need: namely, to integrate the element of water from the unconscious, whereby air would have to retreat somewhat. With such a strong duality on all fronts, we see a horoscope full of turmoil, with possibilities ranging from instability to great creativity. In actuality, both instability and creativity came to the surface at times.

To what extent are we able to speak of an easy or a difficult horoscope here? In my opinion, it is impossible to give an answer to this question without objective standards or criteria. Any answer would be a value judgment, relative both to ourselves and to the way we see the world. The element and cross division in Marilyn's horoscope definitely shows a tense picture, but these same tensions often lead to creativity and great deeds, owing to that unfulfilled feeling which flows through everything as a silent undercurrent.

How the element tension takes concrete form becomes evident when the rest of the horoscope is considered. The greatest care must be exercised in interpretation. Anything indicating further duality between psychic contents must be scrutinized carefully, since this duality shows so clearly through Marilyn's element and cross division. For the more advanced student, it is perhaps significant to point out that neither Uranus nor Pluto make a major aspect in Marilyn's horoscope. When a planet doesn't make any major aspect, it may indicate that the psychic content the planet symbolizes can work in an uncontrolled and uncoordinated way, whereby the planet can unexpectedly exhibit traits of either its most difficult or its best side. The lack of aspects means there is no argument or stress, but also no stimulus from other planets. The unaspected planet represents a psychic content that can work autonomously within the total psyche. Marilyn's horoscope has two such autonomous planets, Uranus and Pluto, both of which are in water signs. Water is precisely the unconscious element whose counteractions her consciousness must try to keep within bounds. Planets located in that inferior element give us further indications about the source of counteractions. The planets Uranus and Pluto, which are by nature

Figure 3.2. Marilyn Monroe. For this discussion the element and cross totals are also included.

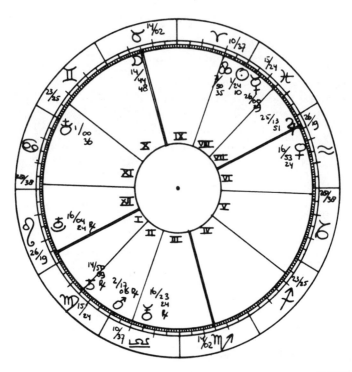

Element	Signs	Houses	Total
FIRE	☉ ♋ Asc.	—	3
EARTH	☽ Mc. ♄	☽ ♄ ♂ ♀	7
AIR	♂ ♋ ♀ ♃	♋ ♃ ♋	7
WATER	♄ ☿	☿ ☉ ♋	5

Crosses	Signs	Houses	Total
CARDINAL	☉ ♋ ♂ ♋	♃ ☽	6
FIXED	☽ Mc. ♋ Asc. ♀ ♃	♄ ♂ ☿ ☉ ♋	11
MUTABLE	♄ ☿	♋ ♀ ♋	5

all but unpredictable for consciousness, are active here from the unconscious inferior element, and moreover are *unaspected*. With such an accumulation of factors, we can say that Marilyn's horoscope tended to become unbalanced. This horoscope shows how important the division of elements and crosses can be for any further interpretation. If, for instance, Uranus and Pluto had been located in air without major aspect, their autonomous actions would not have been so directly threatening to consciousness as they were in Marilyn's case.

The third horoscope, Peter in Chart 3, shows us an example where element is strong enough to be separated out. Figure 3.3 includes Chart 3 and figure 1.8 from Chapter 1, as well as figure 2.5 from Chapter 2, so the reader has easy access to Peter's information now under discussion. The cross division shows considerably fewer difficulties than Marilyn's. In this horoscope, there is also a considerable element tension, in this case from the broad element distribution combined with the fact that the most essential planet— his Aries Sun—is located in an element that doesn't get a chance to express itself in house position. The element opposite the Sun— earth—receives a greater house emphasis. Water, with the personal planet Mercury located in Pisces, also receives the Sun by house position (the eighth house), so that the element of water will increase in importance as Peter grows older. Water has a strongly occupied air element as its opposite. Naturally, every horoscope shows tension. There is no ideal division, just as there are no ideal human beings, but the degree to which a division shows tension can be discerned by looking at a horoscope.

As we said earlier, Peter has the possibility of making a complete change, so that his consciousness would no longer be determined by the potentially strong fire element, but could express a fire/water or even an earth/water combination. The crosses must give us further clarification here. The fixed cross, strongly represented in both potential and circumstances, surpasses the cardinal cross, and surpasses the mutable cross to an even greater degree. This has already caused insistent inner demands in his younger years, as well as when he grows older, so that he feels strongly compelled to

Figure 3.3. Peter's chart. For this discussion the element and cross totals are included.

satisfy these demands and adapt to his unconscious. This means that earth, the probable inferior element in his horoscope, will continually be brought to the surface through psychic energy. Despite the fact that he is an Aries, the combination of the fixed cross and the earth element will help him to display a remarkable amount of tenacity. The possibility, already shown in potential, of making a psychic changeover is confirmed by the cross division. Through the fixed cross, he is so strongly confronted with his own unconscious contents and faculties, that by blending conscious and unconscious elements, a changeover can easily take place, for he would follow the way of least inner resistance. The development of the element division is further completed by the cross division. From this development, we can conclude which points in the horoscope will be of importance before or after the possible change.

As long as Peter experiences life from his element of consciousness—fire—he will be better able to express himself via his Leo Ascendant than via his Taurus Midheaven. As soon as he tends toward earth, because of his element division, his Midheaven will appear more clearly, but at the same time his Ascendant, located in the opposite element, will offer much less support.

Because the possibility of changing the superior element seems to exist within this horoscope, it is also possible to discuss the trend Peter will follow. Despite the carelessness and rashness of the fire element, especially indicated by his Aries Sun, he will develop from a spontaneous individual, jumping from one subject to another, into a person oriented toward a social position in which security and praise (Taurus Moon on the Midheaven) will play a large role. This would be his way of changing from Ascendant to the Midheaven. Of course, in Western culture it is natural that position in society becomes more important as we grow older. We are speaking less, however, about this natural social process than about the fact that Peter's inner experience will eventually express itself in a manner indicated by the Midheaven rather than the Ascendant, which he has followed up until this time. His career would come to mean everything to him, and he would identify with it to such a degree that any change in it or its termination could bring about a huge identity crisis. If he maintains fire as the superior element, the Leo Ascendant would remain important; consequently an end to his career might have a much less radical consequence.

3. A NEW EXAMPLE

In order to show once more the total process of deriving and interpreting the elements and crosses, we will use a new horoscope as an example. Before we can list the elements, look at Paul's horoscope (Chart 4) on page 86. The element division (figure 3.4) and the division of the crosses (figure 3.5) are both on page 87.

Before we begin interpretation, we need to make a few remarks. In this horoscope, we apply the rule pertaining to planets within orb of a house cusp (see Chapter 1, Section 3). The Sun is located at 18° 56′ Cancer, while the ninth house begins at 19° 38′ Cancer. The Sun is located within three degrees of the cusp of the ninth house, so that according to the rule referred to in Chapter 1, the Sun is counted as being in the ninth house. The Sun will be listed in a fire house (in circumstances), which is also a mutable house according to the crosses. If we forgot this rule, we would then derive a completely different element and cross division, even more crucial in the Sun's case since it pertains to such an essential part of the horoscope.

The Midheaven, located at 29° 23′ Leo, *remains* in Leo and does not move to the next sign. A planet close to a house *cusp* may be entered in the following house under certain conditions, but this never applies to a planet, the Midheaven or Ascendant when it is on the cusp of another sign. The Midheaven in this chart is located in the last degree of Leo, so Leo is still decisive. We cannot say that the Midheaven is actually located in Virgo.

When we begin to examine the division of the elements more carefully, the strong occupation of the element water by sign strikes us right away. In no other element are there so many personal planets. By house position, the personal planets Mars and Mercury are again found in water, while the Sun is located in fire, an element already fairly well represented by sign. Earth plays a small role, while the element air, on the other hand, is more important, for it contains Moon both by potential (sign) and circumstance (house).

The total picture indicates someone who views and experiences the world through his feeling function: everything he meets in life is judged through his own feeling standards. Central to this is how he experiences himself, whether agreeable or disagreeable, good or bad, beautiful or ugly, etc. He has an intense emotional involvement with his surroundings, although this doesn't necessarily always

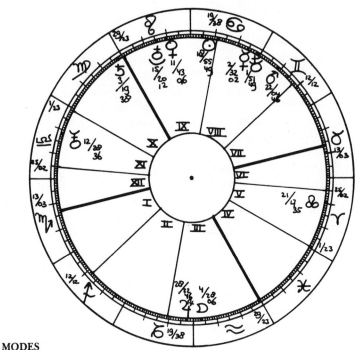

MODES
OR CROSSES:

(6) Cardinal: ♅☿☉♅♃ / ♄

(9) Fixed: ♀♇ MC Asc ☽ / ☿♅♂♅

(7) Mutable: ♂♄ / ♃☽☉♀♇

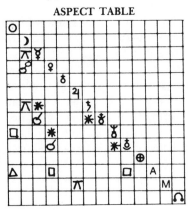

ASPECT TABLE

Sun	☉													
Moon		☽												
Mercury		⚻	☿											
Venus		☍		♀										
Mars					♂									
Jupiter						♃								
Saturn		⚻	✶				♄							
Uranus			☌				✶	♅						
Neptune	□			✶					♆					
Pluto				☌					✶	♇				
Part of Fortune											⊕			
Ascendant	△			□						□		A		
Midheaven						⚻							M	
North Node														☊

ELEMENTS:

Fire: (6)
♀♇ MC / ☉♀♇

Earth: (3)
♄♃ / ♄

Air: (6)
♂♅☽ / ♃☽♅

Water: (7)
♅☿☉ / Asc ♂♅☿

show in his attitude. This is simply the way he sees life and experiences it. He seeks his way through the multiplicity of phenomena with the aid of his feeling function, water.

Since his Moon remains in air, the element contradictory to his superior water element, he will experience a strong tension between his conscious attitude (the Sun) and his unconscious reactions (the Moon). Whenever he is completely involved in further differentiation of his superior feeling function, his Moon will emerge from the unconscious air element, evoking a strong need to arrange everything on a thinking basis. He will prefer to group experiences according to the laws of logic, but this is a weak point since air is clearly his inferior element, working out of his unconscious in a

Potential   *Contents*

Elements	Signs	Houses	Total
FIRE	♀ ♇ Mc.	☉ ♀ ♇	6
EARTH	♄ ♃	♄	3
AIR	♂ ♇ ☽	♃ ☽ ♇	6
WATER	♅ ☉ ☿ Asc.	♂ ♇ ☿	7

Figure 3.4. The elements in Paul's chart.

Crosses	Sign	Houses	Total
CARDINAL	♅ ☿ ☉ ♇ ♃	♄	6
FIXED	♀ ♇ Mc. Asc. ☽	☿ ♅ ♂ ♇	9
MUTABLE	♂ ♄	♃ ☽ ☉ ♀ ♇	7

Figure 3.5. The crosses as expressed in Paul's chart.

Chart 4. Paul's horoscope. He was born in Oosterhout, Holland on July 11, 1949 at 3:30 pm. This birth data is from the birth certificate. House system is Placidus. Chart used with permission.

little-differentiated manner. This doesn't mean that Paul is unable to put order into his experiences. The Moon indicates, among other things, the behavior patterns we unconsciously feel best and most comfortable in pursuing. Because his need for ordering experience is so strong, constant practice in this area will help him draw many significant conclusions. Yet he will find that relying on his feeling ability is much easier and gives him the same results as when he keeps plodding along, deliberately weighing logical factors.

At this point, the cross division becomes important. The strong emphasis which both the cardinal and fixed cross receive by sign gives Paul a fairly good balance between his adaptation to demands from the outside world and demands from his own inner self. In this adaptation, the Moon is active from the fixed sign Aquarius. Therefore, in potential, he will feel the need to direct himself to the Moon's demands. Because the Moon shifts to a mutable house in circumstances, Paul will be increasingly able to use the personal contents of the Moon (unconsciously) as a means of restoring or maintaining balance. The Moon becomes an instrument for him to direct his psychic energy temporarily inwards or outwards. Since we are dealing with a combination of factors in this horoscope, we must consider several things:

a) The superior element is water, which means that air is inferior.

b) Planets located in the inferior air element are active from the unconscious, mostly expressing themselves in the form of counter-actions directed at consciousness. Of the greatest importance here is the fact that the Moon is active within that inferior element.

c) The Moon, as such, indicates how we unconsciously behave in order to feel at ease or to experience a certain form of security. Since this mechanism is active from the inferior air element in this horoscope, the Moon will try to satisfy its own demands even more compulsively. This means Paul will try to understand and explain (as logically as possible) what he is actually perceiving and experiencing through his superior feeling function.

d) In potential, the fixed cross as well as the cardinal cross are strongly occupied, with a focus on the Moon. Therefore, in the first part of his life, Paul will very likely obey the inner compulsive demands of his unconscious Moon. This adaptation will come more naturally to him as he grows older, since the Moon is located in a mutable house in circumstances.

e) The mutable cross receives by far the most house emphasis (circumstances) while the cardinal cross hardly appears. The strong cardinal sign potential, which makes outside impulses the most important for Paul, therefore shifts over to mutable and fixed houses. When we consider all these factors, we come to a conclusion. One of the strongest factors of the unconscious, the Moon, shifts into the mutable cross and begins to play a role in the psyche's process of inner and outer adaptation. Nevertheless, through its location in the inferior element the Moon will maintain a strong connection with the unconscious and with regressive energy. The cardinal cross all but disappears in circumstances, causing the mutable energy to proceed more in the direction of the fixed cross, reemphasizing the fixed potential of the Aquarian Moon.

We have especially concentrated on the Moon to show that one of the greatest values of the element and cross division is the possibility it offers as an indication of certain tension-arousing points in the horoscope. Despite its location in the unconscious, the Moon definitely plays a key role here. In any further interpretation, we must pay special attention to the Moon and its aspects, particularly since the Moon is the dispositor of Paul's Sun in Cancer and therefore of the three planets located in that sign! In spite of the rather placid distribution of the other elements, the Moon is able to dominate consciousness (at least temporarily) and the element of water, so that there appears to be a temporary shift of conscious functions.

The fire element offers the possibility of forming a bridge between air and water in this horoscope. The potential is already sufficient for that purpose, with Venus, Pluto and the Midheaven in fire signs, though it is primarily the house positions that make this balance possible. If he takes advantage of the opportunities offered by his horoscope, on the basis of the element and cross division, Paul probably lives completely through his feelings, while he assumes that he evaluates everything very abstractly and logically. His need for logic, however, is a driving force behind his search for values which he will primarily evaluate emotionally. Despite his logic, it won't be thinking alone that helps him recognize inconsistency, but rather a clear feeling that something might be wrong. This is the combination of water as superior function and fire as auxiliary function of consciousness. His initial need to direct himself to the outer world (the cardinal cross) gradually shifts towards adaptation to whatever he experiences as necessary. Inner values will be decisive more and more frequently (the fixed signs and houses), while the psychic energy processes will become more flexible as he grows older.

The concrete and material will not play a significant role in Paul's life, because the element earth does very little in this horoscope. This doesn't mean Paul will live like a hermit; it only indicates that the material, perceptible, form of things as such won't interest him. It will only play a role within his need for feeling evaluation (water). Furthermore, as the fire element develops further, the earth element will recede into more unconscious levels, being contradictory to the fire element. Its counteractions from the unconscious can contribute to inner balance and help him stand with two feet on the ground through confrontations. This becomes a beneficial counterpart to the strong theorizing need of the Aquarian Moon and the fire element's lack of roots in the earth.

4. PHASES OF LIFE IN THE FRAMEWORK OF CROSS AND ELEMENT

In previous sections, we have repeatedly seen how the division of the elements and crosses develops within the individual psyche. This development is closely connected with age. Naturally, the exact age when changes will take place in an individual can never be given precisely, but there are definite phases of life recognized by both psychology and astrology where much is going on inwardly. Puberty and the change of life in mdidle age are well-known phases with characteristic developments that everyone goes through.

When interpreting a horoscope, we definitely need to take these ages into account. If we are to interpret a horoscope having strong air sign occupation, for instance, we can hardly speak of a well-developed thinking function if the horoscope is that of a small child! We can say that the child will gradually orient himself on the basis of the thinking function. Thinking will be rather simple and uncontrolled in the beginning, but, as the child grows older, many original and archaic traits disappear as a result of increasing differentiation. It could well be the case that there is a strong air potential (planets in the air signs) yet few planets in air houses (circumstances). Sooner or later the child would discover that his thinking faculty, well-developed as it may be, isn't always sufficient. Other functions or other elements would play a more important role than if there had been planets located in air houses. This problem would make itself felt at some time in his life, with all the possibilities and difficulties it offers.

One of the most important periods in a person's life is the crisis of middle age, which generally takes place between age forty-two and forty-five. Astrologically speaking, transiting Saturn, transiting Uranus, and the secondary progressed Moon each form an opposition with their own natal position.[2] The structure and contents of life are then ready for great changes. C.A. Meier says the following about this crisis:

> ...sooner or later, but normally speaking around the middle of life, the wheel of functions begins to turn. What has received the main emphasis up until then gradually becomes less important, and what was despised, then appears to full advantage...[3]

When the unconscious contents belonging to the inferior function can no longer be repressed they demand our attention, creating a crisis. Astrologically, we can say the following: in the first half of life it is primarily the potential—the planets in the signs—that is decisive for the individual. This is particularly important during childhood, especially in puberty, when the formation of the ego is important. Astrologically, during this phase the emphasis falls on the Sun. The influence of the planets in the houses generally becomes noticeable during this period. Little by little, the individual accumulates more experience, learns how to assimilate and comprehend more, and involuntarily his circumstances will be incorporated into this inner process of learning and adaptation.

In most cases, the influence of the planets in the houses seems to become more intense in the late twenties. At that time both the

---

[2] See *Astro-Psychology* for details.

[3] Meier, C.A., *Bewusstsein*. Erkenntnistheorie und Bewusstsein. Bewusstwerdung bei C.G. Jung, Wather Verlag, Olten, 1975, p. 140.

secondary progressed Moon, and transiting Saturn, have made one complete circle through the zodiac, returning to their place in the birth horoscope. Astrologically we call this the first Moon-Saturn return.[4] From this period on, one is more clearly and consciously confronted with circumstances through experiences. In the end, this comes down to a constant confrontation with the self. A person may learn a great deal about unknown factors which are actually part of his own unconscious, if he is prepared to pay attention to how he spontaneously reacts to things that come his way. This phase culminates around the middle of life. Both potential and circumstances (sign and house) are very strongly in evidence, and in regard to the elements in the horoscope, begin to fuse at that time. Potential can never completely be suppressed, but becomes more subtle in many cases.

When we are looking at the horoscope of someone just graduating from school, we should discuss it more on an element level, emphasizing the possible tendencies for development. Someone who is middle-aged already has a certain record, and we must take into account that tendencies have largely materialized; one can speak of a furthering differentiation in which the unconscious counteractions have already played a greater role. For instance, if the person has an earth emphasis, we can be confident that the fire contents have hardly come into play. The fire contents will make themselves more clearly felt at middle age, and therefore changes in consciousness may come about. These changes are all the more likely if the strongest element by sign comes off worse by house. It is then possible that the person will develop a strong auxiliary function or even turn this into a superior function. A person can even become exactly the opposite type, with the understanding that the inferior function, in becoming superior, will partially differentiate itself but will never completely lose the traits it originally possessed in the unconscious. It is also very possible that someone has lived for a long time with a function that doesn't suit him. In that case, a shift to a function that *does* suit him may take place in the middle of life. This kind of radical shift especially can take place in an unbalanced element division.

---

[4]For literature about the phases of life, see footnote 2 in Chapter 2. Astrologically, see Robertson, M., *Critical Ages in Adult Life: The Transit of Saturn*, American Federation of Astrologers, Inc. 1976.

The crosses play an important role here as well. The world outside will continue to play an important role for someone with a strong cardinal cross, for instance. In that case, consciousness is directed toward adapting to outer demands. Inner demands are denied, neglected, or hardly felt. When the transition years arrive and the unconscious increases its demands, a person with a strong cardinal cross (in potential and circumstances) can be severely troubled although he may prefer not to show this to the outside world!

This midlife crisis plays a much slighter role for someone with many planets emphasized in the fixed element. All his life, even if unconsciously, he will have been absorbed in the demands of his inner world. From an early age, he probably has been confronted with himself, and he is somewhat accustomed to the intrusion of his unconscious upon consciousness. For him, a different sort of shift will take place in the middle of life. Naturally, this must be examined in connection to the elements.

The mutable cross can go in various directions in the mid-life crisis. Because this cross has to do with transitional situations (from progresson to regression and vice versa), awarenesss of the actual direction of psychic energy may elude a person with a strong mutable cross. Perhaps because of this, the person may not even be aware that he has landed in a crisis, although he may be able to realize it afterwards. When the mutable cross is especially strong in a horoscope, without any appreciable occupation of the cardinal and fixed signs, then the transition of elements will probably take place smoothly, though the actual experiencing of the change occurs later. In the most positive form, the person with mutables strong by sign and house can remain neutral towards himself and others, thus not making the times more difficult than they already are.

When interpreting a horoscope, we must continually consider the phase of life being experienced. The exact division of the elements and the crosses then indicates:

a) The direct potential: planets in the signs.

b) The degree to which one can give form to this potential in the circumstances: planets in the houses.

c) The manner of assimilation: the cross division in potential.

d) The degree to which one experiences the opposition between consciousness and the unconscious: the division of the element pairs;

e) The degree to which this changes as one grows older: the element division concerning the houses in regard to the signs.

f) The degree to which the occupation of the signs and houses can cause tension by the element division.

g) How the assimilation process initially takes place: the cross division in potential, and:

h) How the assimilation process crystallizes, becomes more refined and develops further: the crosses in circumstances.

i) How the assimilation process and functions of consciousness (the crosses and the elements, respectively) can support or oppose each other in the course of one's life.

The instinctive process is still foremost in childhood. During that time, consciousness becomes further crystallized through learning, until preliminary completion takes place around the age of thirty. Only at the time of the midlife crisis can elements and crosses be interpreted in their totality for consciousness; in other words, potential and experience only begins to blend at that time, through which a new personality can begin to develop. Naturally, there are exceptions to the rule. When, because of horoscope structure, someone has dealt with certain progressions related to the psyche at a very young age, and these have been accompanied by profound and drastic experiences, there will be a quickening of the general processes of life, even though the general human tendency still exists.

The division of crosses and elements in the individual horoscope must be closely examined, in the light of personality structure, phase of life, and experience. When we have considered all that, with the help of the division alone, we can discern the problems of someone going through midlife crisis. In the same manner, we can often recognize the major problems of other phases of life. In any case, we must continue to take into account the general psychic significance of the phase, evaluating the role of the elements and the crosses against this background.[5]

[5]For literature about the phases of life, see footnote 2 in Chapter 2. Astrologically, see Robertson, M., *Critical Ages in Adult Life: The Transit of Saturn,* American Federation of Astrologers, Inc. 1976.

Chapter Four

Personal Planets
Within the Element and Cross Division

1. The Castle

While making the element and cross divisions, we learned that the very personal contents—the Sun, Moon, Mercury, and Ascendant—play an important role, since a large part of everybody's framework is directly connected with these components of the psyche. The Ascendant, Sun, Moon, and other planets each play an independent role within the element and cross divisions in addition. Therefore, it is important to know to what extent the contents (or planets) agree with or differ from the basic framework. Countless processes are going on in a horoscope, and it is not always easy to see what is happening internally from anyone's outward behavior and appearance. A person can seem to be in harmony yet have considerable inner conflict. Similarly, a person may seem to have many problems, while inwardly being hardly troubled by anything. The horoscope can reveal much concerning the difference between appearance and reality. The following example may illustrate the relationship between what someone shows the outside world and what lies hidden according to the horoscope.

Let us imagine the horoscope as a huge, unknown castle that we are approaching. In the distance, as we ride up to the building, we first see a large tower with a flag on top. This represents the M.C. (the Midheaven or the beginning of the tenth house). This point in the horoscope indicates the ego-image: that with which we identify ourselves—our flag, in other words—and the status in society connected with this image. The closer our approach to the castle, the more we notice the outside of the building, until we find ourselves standing right before it, on the point of entering. We can only enter the castle by means of a drawbridge and the portal, which can be compared to the entrance and exit of the horoscope—the Ascendant. The drawbridge gives us our first impression of the castle, just as we receive an impression of a new acquaintance through the Ascendant (and thereby the whole first house). This drawbridge may have all sorts of iron fixtures, snags, clasps, trapdoors, and the like, creating an unpleasant impression or seemingly wanting to keep us at a distance. However, the whole castle isn't necessarily furnished in that manner. No matter how much the drawbridge forms part of the castle, it is but one of its many components. Behind this frightening drawbridge, very possibly we will find a most charming and romantic little castle where we could feel quite at home. If we discover this to be so, then we will view the drawbridge (the Ascendant) with very different eyes. Nevertheless, we may be startled at the sight of it.

Astrologically, the Ascendant reflects a person's natural way of acting, his habitual external behavior, and his way of responding to new impulses and impressions. By the Ascendant, we mean not only the cusp of the first house, but also the planets forming angles to it. If the Ascendant has many difficult aspects, the person may seem to be rather difficult, even though a good deal of balance and harmony may be present in the rest of the horoscope. It is equally possible that the Ascendant receives only harmonious aspects, so that the person, despite great conflicts in the rest of the chart, seems to have few conflicts. Our first acquaintance with the Ascendant may be extremely deceptive, if we make a judgement on this basis alone. Yet, we must not forget that the drawbridge fulfills a very essential role for the castle, and this is true for the Ascendant with regard to the rest of the horoscope as well. The Ascendant definitely represents a certain character trait, but it is not the only one. The planets, the aspects, the relation between the houses, and so forth, determine what the rest of the castle looks like. It may turn out to be a castle containing many tastefully and pleasantly furnished rooms, or it may, for instance, consist of very separate sections. Since the planets in the inferior element can bring hidden and gnawing contents to light, we also may learn the cellar in our castle is full of mice and rats. Just as we explore the castle from within, we learn to know the horoscope from within. Then we see how compatible the Ascendant and Midheaven really are with the person, and to what extent the flag covers the cargo.

From this comparison, it may be seen that our first impression will agree more with the person's character if the Ascendant corresponds with the element and cross division of the horoscope than if the Ascendant deviates from the rest of the picture. Someone having a strongly occupied earth element and a strong fixed cross, for instance, will not seem as he actually is if his Ascendant is Gemini (air). The volatility and lightheartedness of this Ascendant would conceal the calmer and steadier character, so the outwardly directed Gemini Ascendant would be misleading. The fixed cross would indicate a person who primarily abides by his own standards. Yet the Ascendant (his natural and direct way of acting) will give his character mutability as a beneficial counterpart to strong regressive tendencies. On the other hand, this can pose a problem, since he seems to unite two characters in one person through this duality. One part continually needs to digest and assimilate experience, while the other part throws itself once more into all kinds of things that are not wholly assimilated (Gemini!), so quickly that the first can't cope with it.

The Ascendant plays a very unique role within the horoscope. It reflects the psychic content that determines how we manifest ourselves outwardly. It is an important part of our character, sometimes so natural that when people call attention to the traits we will have trouble recognizing them. Only when we have carefully observed ourselves for awhile will Ascendant characteristics become clear to us. The inward reaction pattern indicated by the Ascendant is also reflected in reactions to immediate physical circumstances. The Ascendant therefore shows both our direct reaction to intangible things such as experiences and events, and our way of reacting to tangible circumstances such as climate.

2. THE SUN IN THE DIVISION OF TYPES

Opinions vary as to the role played by the Sun in the horoscope. Some consider the Sun equal in importance to the other contents of the horoscope, while others give it a special place since it is the most direct reflection of our essence and our ego. Sooner or later the Sun will make itself felt, no matter how concealed it is. It is concealed in a house where it can't express itself clearly, such as the twelfth, or if it is unaspected. The person is then barely able to express his own nature and essence in his circumstances, while feeling these contents strongly within himself.

In my opinion, the Sun plays a very important role in the horoscope. Sooner or later, it is the point to which we unconsciously wish to return when we have strayed from the path it indicates. One can speak about straying from the path of the Sun in the case of those who orient themselves to the element contradictory to their superior element (often that is the element in which the Sun is located). In psychology, the problem of this 'disturbed type' is represented by M.-L. von Franz as follows:

> ...Some people have trouble in finding out their own type, which very often is due to the fact that they are distorted types. This is not a very frequent occurrence, but it does happen in cases where someone would naturally have become a feeling type or an intuitive, but was forced by the surrounding atmosphere to develop another function. Suppose a boy is born a feeling type in an intellectually ambitious family. His surroundings will exert pressure upon him to become an intellectual, and his original predisposition as a feeling type will be thwarted or despised. Usually, in such a case, he is unable to become a thinking type: that would be one step too far. But he might well develop sensation or intuition, one of the auxiliary functions, so as to be relatively better adapted to his surroundings; his main function is simply 'out' in the milieu in which he grows up.[1]

Peter's horoscope (Chart 3) illustrates von Franz's ideas. His family led an upright existence according to Christian standards, held traditional thought patterns, and considered a social career an honorable pursuit. Peter, with his Aries Sun and Leo Ascendant both in fire, had trouble with this upbringing at an early age. He

---

[1]von Franz, M.-L. and J. Hillman, *Lectures on Jung's Typology*, Spring Verlag, Zürich, 1971, Part 1, p. 3.

had a strong need for inner freedom and self-expression, but because the Moon is located in earth (Taurus), he also had a strong need for security which is contrary to his fire Sun. In his case, the prominent earth-water houses clearly reflect his childhood environment, in which feeling, tradition, and security formed the pillars of the family. The circumstances that Peter grew up in meant he wasn't able to give full scope to his fire contents, although his parents were very cooperative in allowing him to develop himself.

At twelve years of age, he was introduced to the idea of missionary training; he let himself be talked into it and went to a seminary. He missed his home (Moon in Taurus) but enjoyed the possibilities and perspectives this training offered (fire signs). Within that environment, he gained prestige and belonged to the grown-up men. Yet, it didn't turn out to be what he was actually seeking; and, after a number of years, he terminated this study to begin a university education. To the great sorrow of his parents, he said farewell to the church.

During those study years, he indulged his potentially strong fire traits: the Sun doesn't allow itself to be repressed, especially when other contents, for instance the Leo Ascendant, are located in the same element. Yet the emphasis on the Sun gradually diminished and the water element became more prominent, which can be seen in a need to express himself artistically. Earth began to play a stronger role as well, although with difficulty, since it is an inferior element. His largely unconscious need for security will play an increasingly greater role in his life (strong earth houses). Indeed, we may say that upbringing and childhood environment are still working unconsciously, but if the fire houses had been stronger, the effect of childhood years may have been quite different. At birth, there was a predisposition for these experiences and for the tendencies of further development. The large role played by earth element in his psyche is strengthened by the fixed cross, which constantly brings the inferior earth element to the surface.

In the preceding chapter, we pointed out the strong possibility of making a changeover in this horoscope. In fact, a change already took place in youth, namely from traditional Christian to noncon-formist and non-churchgoer. This meant breaking away from the parental environment. Nevertheless, the battle between fire and earth will always remain important for him. This can mean that another period may occur in which earth becomes more important than fire, probably bridged by the water element. This changeover doesn't have to be lasting; rather, we can see him balancing on the razor's edge trying to keep his balancing through a strong auxiliary function—the element of water.

Von Franz has the following to say about the disadvantages of the distorted type:

> ...from the very beginning they cannot develop their main disposition; they therefore remain a bit below the mark they would have reached had they developed in the one-sided way. On the other hand they have been forced ahead of time into doing something which in the second half of life they would have had to do anyway...[2]

The intense confrontation with the inferior function, which forms the crisis around ages forty-two to forty-five, will mean that Peter will be going through something that he has known for a long time. All his life he has been wrestling with this duality, which is at the same time the source of his creativity. At that time, he may again make a temporary changeover, but in all probability his difficulties will not increase.

The fire element will continue to play a role in his new direction in life—music—a career which came after his university studies. He will probably continue to search for new possibilities and ways of expression within his existing framework. The storminess will gradually disappear and make room for more earth and (primarily) water contents to express. Peter is one example that shows how important the Sun is in element division. To the degree that the element division becomes more imbalanced, the Sun will more often be decisive, whether or not it forms any aspects or whether they are easy or difficult according to traditional astrological standards.

3. Consciousness and the Moon

By using the concept *consciousness* as defined in Chapter 1, we can better understand that the astrological content of the Moon, so

[2]*Ibid.*, p. 4.

closely interwoven with the unconscious, can also play an important role for consciousness. The Moon is a very personal content; it
represents unconscious learned behavior, part of our past and our
youth, and above all indicates the way we behave in order to feel
comfortable or the attitude in which we feel best. Most astrologers
agree that this attitude is of an unconscious origin. When these
contents are brought to the attention of the ego through the function
of consciousness, then the ego can have a much better image of its
own psyche than when the contents of the Moon remain hidden,
provided the ego accepts these contents as from itself. Someone, for
instance, having a strong Gemini emphasis is very much involved in
surroundings. This person wants to participate in everything,
experience everything, and know and talk about it. In short,
excitement and liveliness appeal a great deal. If someone had Moon
in Pisces, unconscious enjoyment by withdrawing into peace and
quiet to catch one's breath, not actively participating for a while, no
matter how much a desire to participate is also part of the character,
would be a part of the personality. This inner duality can be
experienced as troublesome for the individual may try to identify
with one of the two sides. However, this always leads to increased
tension, since both contents are present and both pull on the psyche
to be recognized. If the individual doesn't allow personal seclusion
now and then, the ego fails to appreciate the contents of the Pisces
Moon. The result is that the individual is less conscious than if a
willing comprehension of both sides of character were recognized.
The realization of the Moon can increase awareness and make a
more balanced self-image. It may sound paradoxical that unconscious contents can also contribute to the broadening of our field of
consciousness. It will be self-evident, however, that in order to
broaden, expand, and deepen consciousness, certain components are
necessary that we weren't conscious of before. We are hereby
thinking of an expansion of consciousness in regard to components
the ego can easily identify with or wishes to enrich itself with, as
well as a deepening of consciousness in regard to components the
ego could not or did not want to accept or comprehend before.

Perhaps we may restate the way the elements work on the whole
psyche: consciousness passes information onto the ego, which
filters it, *i.e.* assimilates, forgets, or represses the information. The
way consciousness passes on information is indicated by the

elements, while the crosses indicate the way assimilation or repression takes place afterwards. The role of the Sun, emphasized in the preceding section, can be clarified within the theory of consciousness: the Sun represents the ego or the self in the horoscope.

4. MERCURY AND CONSCIOUSNESS

Mercury is the planet that connects everything—facts, information, people, and things from the outer world, as well as contents from the inner world. Mercury is also considered one of the personal planets. It has a specific meaning in the relationship between consciousness and the unconscious since it maintains the interaction of contents and information from both. It can connect the Sun and Moon, and at the same time bring the Sun and Moon into contact with the outside world. In this way, the element in which Mercury is located plays a subtle role in the organization of consciousness. Strikingly, where there is a great conflict between the Sun and Moon, if the Sun is active in the superior and the Moon in the inferior element, Mercury's element will become prominent. In Peter's horoscope, (see Chart 3 on page 42), this is the case. The Sun in Aries and Moon in Taurus produces a fire-earth duality. Through Mercury's location in Pisces, water comes into prominence, to a much greater degree than Venus (also personal) does in the air element.

It is extremely difficult to give exact rules that would apply to each horoscope. Each horoscope has its own unique combination which demands that it be examined with all its own nuances. Nevertheless, the Sun, Moon, Mercury, and Ascendant deserve special attention in the element and cross divisions, as illustrated by the above remarks.

Chapter Five

Sample Horoscopes

1. Background

For the last several chapters we have been discussing how the planets and houses affect the personality in relation to the elements and crosses within the horoscope. For the sake of taking this discussion further, we will now examine three different horoscopes to see how the energy manifests.

People who are born at the same time and in the same place are called astro-twins in astrology. This happens only when two people are born at the same hour and at the same longitude and latitude. When this occurs, the lives of the two people will be strikingly similar. A similar circumstance can also occur when more than one person is born at the same Greenwich Time. In other words, although the location of the birth is different, the Greenwich Time used to calculate the planetary positions is the same. And to take this idea a step further, there are relationships and differences between people who are born at the same Greenwich Time, but in a different location. When such circumstances arise, a person will share Greenwich Time with another person, but the houses will be very different because the people involved were born in different places on the earth.

The individual with the same planetary positions, but with a different set of houses—meaning that the Ascendant and Midheaven would be different—create an interesting experiment for us to interpret, for we can see how the element and cross divisions would

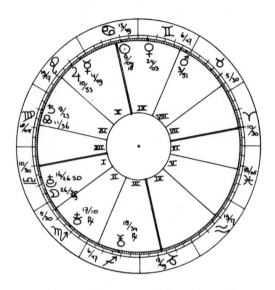

Chart 5. An imaginary chart created for Amsterdam.

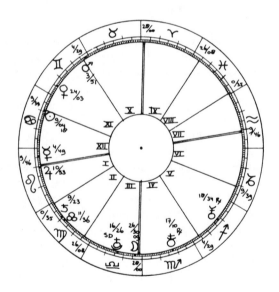

Chart 6. The same data as used in Chart 5, with the houses calculated for New York City as the birthplace.

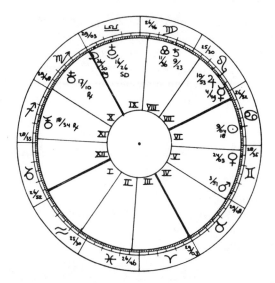

Chart 7. The same planets in Chart 5 and 6, but with the houses calculated as if Djaharta, Java was the birthplace.

affect such personalities. For the sake of a learning experience, I have provided totally imaginary horoscopes (Charts 5, 6, and 7). These three horoscopes have the same planets, but have been calculated for different cities. The change in birth location shows us three different people, who will express their natal energy through very different element and cross divisions as we shall see.

If all three people should become interested in astrology, they would read exactly the same interpretations in reference books: the Sun in Cancer indicates this, the Moon in Libra indicates that, and so on. The aspects between the planets will also be identical. However, the aspects to the Ascendant and Midheaven, as well as the house positions of the planets, indicating areas of experience, will differ. Because of this, they will become very different people, even though they share many characteristics. Their areas of experience will differ, and, therefore, their possible development and difficulties. On the basis of these differences, certain planets will appear more clearly in one horoscope than in another, as will be seen when we analyze the division of the elements and crosses. Try to answer some questions in regard to these horoscopes:

1. What does the division of the crosses and elements for each of
    the three horoscopes look like?
2. Are there notable differences between the horoscopes?
3. Briefly, how would we interpret the division in Chart 5?
4. What can be said about Chart 6?
5. What about Chart 7?

2. NOTABLE DIFFERENCES BETWEEN THE CHARTS

In comparing the element division in Charts 5, 6, and 7 (see fig. 5.1),
there are distinct differences that can be pointed out. Naturally, a
number of points will be identical: the planets are located in the
same signs in all three charts and therefore they will be the same in
potential for the element divisions. The Ascendant and the
Midheaven, however, are not alike. In Chart 6, the fire element
receives enormous emphasis because the Midheaven and Ascendant
are located in that element potential. This is not the case in Charts 5
and 7. In potential, therefore, Chart 6 deviates sharply from the
other two.

A comparison of the circumstances (planets in the houses)
reveals some notable differences. Chart 5, for instance has few
possibilities to manifest the water element (in which the Sun is
located!) by house, although the strongly-developing fire element
can be of help since it doesn't conflict with the water element. Like
water, the air element, equally strong by sign, has little possibility to
express itself in house position. The water-air duality plays a clear
role by sign (even more so since both the Ascendant and Midheaven
are concerned), but it disappears almost completely by house
position (circumstances). It gives way to a total fire predominance in
which Mercury in Leo (out of an earth house) causes a duality in
circumstances.

In Chart 6, fire is strongly developed by sign (potential), having
Mercury, the Leo Ascendant and Aries Midheaven as its personal
contents. The air-water duality also plays a role, although less
strongly than in Chart 5 where the Ascendant and Midheaven were
contributing. In contrast to Chart 5, Chart 6 can express itself well
in circumstances: water is strongly emphasized, fire and air
somewhat less, while earth remains in the background. The

a) Chart 5

Elements	Signs	Houses	Total
FIRE	☿ ♃ ♅	☊ ☽ ♂ *♀ ☉	8
EARTH	♄	♆ ☿ ♃	4
AIR	♂ ♀ Asc. ☊ ☽	♅ ♄	7
WATER	☉ Mc. ♆	—	3

b) Chart 6

Elements	Signs	Houses	Total
FIRE	☿ ♃ Asc. Mc. ♅	♃ ♅	7
EARTH	♄	♄	2
AIR	♂ ♀ ☊ ☽	☊ ♂ *♀	7
WATER	☉ ♆	☽ *♆ ☉ ☿	6

c) Chart 7

Elements	Signs	Houses	Total
FIRE	☿ ♃ ♅	♂ ♀ ☊	6
EARTH	♄ Asc.	☉ ☽ *♆	5
AIR	♂ ♀ ☊ ☽ Mc.	☿ ♃ ♅	8
WATER	☉ ♆	♄	3

Figure 5.1. As you will notice, the element division for a, b and c differ a great deal. Even though these charts were all calculated for the same day, the difference in birthplace has changed the emphasis of the elements. (*Denotes cuspal planets. See page 16.)

character in Chart 6 will develop more and more along the lines of a purely feeling person (water), with fire as an auxiliary function.

Chart 7 differs completely from Charts 5 and 6. Since earth has a strong personal content by sign (potential) due to the Capricorn Ascendant, this element gains more importance than it did in either Chart 5 or 6, and the difference becomes even greater when we relate this to house distribution (circumstance). Although Chart 7 gets little chance of expressing its nature (symbolized by the Sun) by circumstance—only Saturn is located in a water house—earth continually becomes more important, and this is an element that gets along well with the Cancer sun sign. The original duality between water and air shifts in circumstances somewhat, due to fire-earth duality playing a greater role in the house placements. Earth is now actually the strongest (in contrast to Chart 5). Mercury plays a different role: it is located in a fire sign (potential) and expresses itself in an air house (circumstances), an easy combination for this planet. But the basis of the horoscope is the tension between air and water, in which earth can make itself useful as an auxiliary function, but also as a means of escape. With this in mind, Mercury, because of its position in an air house, shares in the primary tension of the horoscope.

As a whole, the charts appear in a different light when we relate them to the cross division. See figure 5.2. We have already seen some large differences in the element division; the cross division indicates how these different attitudes are assimilated inwardly. Charts 5 and 7 both have a strong cardinal cross—besides the Sun and Moon, the Ascendant and Midheaven are located in that cross. Consequently, both horoscopes indicate an assimilation process strongly directed toward adapting to outward norms and values. In both horoscopes, we again find the Sun in a mutable house (circumstances), although the mutable cross is more strongly emphasized in Chart 5 than in 7. The planets located in mutable signs (potential) are located in mutable houses (circumstances) in Chart 5, but all of them are in fixed houses in Chart 7. Taken as a whole, this means that Chart 7 will be more fixed by that cardinal cross than Chart 5, creating a somewhat easier transition and a more flexible formation.

Chart 6 shows a rather broad distribution of the planets within the crosses, and both the cardinal and fixed crosses are well occupied with personal contents. Since the Moon is also located in the

a) Chart 5

Crosses	Signs	Houses	Total
CARDINAL	☉ Mc. Asc. ♅ ☽	♅ ☽ ☿ ♃	9
FIXED	☿ ♃ ♄	♄ ♅	5
MUTABLE	♂ ♀ ♄ ♇	♅ ♂ * ♀ ☉	8

b) Chart 6

Crosses	Signs	Houses	Total
CARDINAL	☉ ♅ ☽ Mc.	♃ ☽ * ♄	7
FIXED	☿ ♃ Asc. ♅	♄ ♅ ♂ ♀	8
MUTABLE	♂ ♀ ♄ ♇	♅ ☉ ☿	7

c) Chart 7

Crosses	Signs	Houses	Total
CARDINAL	☉ ♅ ☽ Asc. Mc.	☿ ♃ ☽ * ♄	9
FIXED	☿ ♃ ♄	♂ ♀ ♄ ♇	7
MUTABLE	♂ ♀ ♄ ♇	☉ ♅	6

Figure 5.2. The division of the crosses changes when we look at Charts 5, 6 and 7. (*Denotes cuspal planets. See page 16.)

---

cardinal cross by house position, this cross remains strong. The fixed cross also acquires Venus and Mars, yet these planets are somewhat less important than the Sun, Moon, Mercury, Ascendant, and Midheaven. The importance of this cross, through the position of the Sun and Mercury in mutable houses, will increase as this person becomes older, so attitude and behavior may show an increasing flexibility. On the other hand, the fixed Ascendant produces a great deal of resistance.

In summary: with regard to the crosses, the distribution is most even in Chart 6, allowing more sides of the personality to be developed. In a very subtle way, however, tension, can also arise. The strong cardinal cross is located diametrically opposite the fixed cross, so the developing mutable cross will need to invest a lot of energy to keep the cardinal and fixed cross in balance.

3. BRIEF INTERPRETATION OF CHART 5

In Chart 5, we can say in potential that this is a feeling person who has difficulty expressing feeling judgments and evaluations of situations because possibilities for expression are lacking in the houses. Moreover, the urge to experience things through feeling (Sun) is strongly influenced by impulses from the air element (Moon, Asc.), so that the balance is shaky. The feeling evaluation of situations continually conflicts with the need to arrange everything mentally and to reflect upon events and situations. The contradiction between the Sun and the Moon unites itself by location in the fire houses with the result that this element probably will play an important role for consciousness at an early age. The shaky sign balance (potential) would cause the influence of the houses to be felt at an early age. Both the need to experience life in a feeling way and the need for logical reasoning can be satisfied by the fire houses. The search for possibilities, the chasing after future dreams, the fiery longings to experience everything, the desire to understand things is expressed through fire. Through this, the intuitive side can develop. Generally, the water element is known for its ability to sense and feel *through* certain situations or events. Fire's support in this horoscope makes possible further development and creates a growing understanding of why things happen. The practical side plays a subordinate role in this, because earth is hardly developed, even though thinking (Mercury) must develop in a concrete house. This Mercury in combination with a strong cardinal cross, can give a certain purposefulness to consciousness, whereby the mutable cross provides the necessary flexibility whenever desired.

Being in a fixed sign, Mercury has a difficult time in this horoscope, since it is connected with unconscious contents that can harass consciousness through the regressive movement of the fixed cross. Thus Mercury has a need for depth, both in thinking and in contacts, but because of its location in a cardinal house, this doesn't always work out. Even though its position in a fire sign is very promising, it must express itself in an earth house. This means the following is taking place in Chart 5:

a) a duality in potential between water and air, which leads to a shaky balance;

b) the fire element provides a good bridge and will continually become more important;

c) the strong cardinal cross energy causes the combination of elements to show an outward directedness: adaptation to the demands of the surroundings;

d) the mutable cross, which becomes stronger with age, makes this adaptation easy and creates smooth transition situations;

e) however, there are two difficult points:

• the element of water, so important for the Cancerian nature, has no possibility of expression, and this can give a gnawing feeling of not being understood, which, by the way, may stimulate this person to express via the fire outlets.

• Mercury is the central point of various conflicting tendencies: it shifts from fixed to cardinal and from fire to earth. Within this structure both the fixed cross need of depth and the fire element need of a variety of possibilities and grand future dreams cannot be secured without an arduous struggle.

4. BRIEF INTERPRETATION OF CHART 6

In Chart 6 (as in Chart 5), you see the duality between air and water. Here, however, the contradiction is not resolved by a strong fire element by house as it was in Chart 5, since it is clear that water houses are predominant here. Fire, it is true, is strongly represented by sign, with Mercury, Ascendant and Midheaven in fire, but it has difficulty realizing its potential by house position (cirumstances). Therefore, the search for possibilities and the reality behind appearances is not as much a means to bridge the duality here as we saw in Chart 5. In this horoscope, fire is much more an essential component of the psyche.

The circumstances this person will experience in a lifetime are those of water, in complete agreement with the Cancer Sun. The Moon, located in an air sign, will have to express itself in a water house as well, like Mercury, which originates in fire. Everything in this horoscope indicates that water, although having a shaky balance with air by sign, will rapidly crystallize into the superior function. Automatically, therefore, air becomes inferior and the occupation of the fire signs in potential makes one suppose that fire will crystallize rather easily into a first auxiliary function.

Because of the equal and balanced distribution of the planets in the crosses, the assimilation process will take place rather smoothly. The person will know how to withdraw in time and when to go ahead, as the moment may require. The cardinal cross has a slight upper hand, so that we may say this is a feeling person needing impulses from the surroundings and adapting accordingly. The goal is the outer world and by means of this the individual can give form to the self.

Through the combination of the strongest element—water—and the slightly predominant cardinal cross, we automatically arrive at the sign of Cancer, the water sign of the cardinal cross. This results in our having to interpret the entire horoscope in the direction of Cancer, despite the fact that only the Sun is found in this sign and even though it is hidden away in the twelfth house.

Of the three, Chart 6 has the basis most fitting with its Sun sign. This has a great advantage for the emotional life which therefore will experience less uncertainty and show fewer ripples on the surface of the water. The planets lying hidden under the surface in the element air, such as Venus and Mars, can call forth strong reactions from the unconscious. The relative harmony predominating in consciousness, therefore, doesn't necessarily apply to the whole psyche. One advantage is a balance in consciousness, but there is also a greater chance that attitudes become rigid, causing the unconscious to become more active and to undertake more counteractions. In this horoscope, we can deduce the direction of this action from the planets located in the air signs.

5. BRIEF INTERPRETATION OF CHART 7

There is an element duality between water and air, and to a small degree between fire (Mercury) and earth (Ascendant). Therefore, a double polarity exists in potential, whereby it is very difficult to determine which element will have the upper hand in Chart 7. There is little doubt about this in circumstances: the earth houses contain the Sun and Moon, thereby receiving the greatest emphasis. Still, Saturn and the Ascendant in earth signs are not sufficient to make this element superior. Through the house emphasis (circumstances), however, earth would eventually become superior in the course of life. By house the water element has difficulty coming into its own; air gets along somewhat better. This results in a continuation of the tension between the very important Sun and the air houses, so that earth can soon develop into an element of escape. In other words, out of a feeling/thinking duality there is a tendency to develop sensation as the main function, with feeling and thinking as auxiliary functions, the way of least resistance in this division. Just as in Chart 5, the essential nature—water—is not quite fulfilled, which can give rise to undirected feelings, such as not being understood. These feelings aren't necessarily expressed verbally; they may float through this person's experience like a haze, influencing behavior and thinking. Through the element of air, thinking will certainly show compulsive traits and can appear in uncontrolled spells; the earth element can be a hindrance in this, at least in an inhibiting way.

If Saturn played an insignificant role in Chart 6, here it becomes very important due to the earth emphasis and its possible development into the superior element. By far, Saturn can express itself best in this horoscope, especially since it doesn't form part of the unconscious as in Charts 5 and 6. Therefore, Chart 7 is much more directed towards the concrete, material, and practical, with an even greater purposefulness than the other two. However, this is partly due to the lack of the intuitive faculty that characterizes Chart 5, for instance.

The crosses show us that assimilation primarily takes place when progressive and mutable energy is addressed by the individual. Only when we view the totality does the fixed cross play a role later on. Strongly geared to the outer world, the cardinal cross has an easier time, since the Sun expresses itself in a mutable house. This doesn't alter the fact that this horoscope shows less flexibility than Chart 6. The mutable cross mainly serves progressive energy, but the fixed cross will continue to make itself felt in a subtle way in that planets in mutable signs must express themselves in fixed houses.

This gives a certain stability but also less flexibility than in the other two. There is already less flexibility on account of the element division, and the stability of earth causes a greater firmness in this case.

6. CONCLUDING REMARKS

From the preceding analysis, it may be seen that even though three people are born on the same day with exactly the same Greenwich Time and therefore exactly the same planet positions, their characters nevertheless will differ essentially because of the differing basis formed by the elements and the crosses. Chart 5 will welcome all possibilities in life as an escape from an inner duality. Chart 6, on the other hand, may spend quite a long time in a world of feelings and dreams created through its strong water potential. Chart 7 will approach life in a practical and concrete manner based on feeling, though more directed than the other two.

Therefore, although these three different horoscopes have the same planets and aspects, when their basis is thoroughly analyzed, one can see that certain planetary aspects will show up more clearly in one than in another. For example, seen in the light of the elements and crosses, the sextile between the Sun and Saturn should be considered more important in Chart 7 than in Chart 5. Every individual is unique, and the division of the elements and crosses in a horoscope indicates the direction in which we must interpret the aspects and significance of the planetary positions we have dealt with in a general way, in order to reconcile their contents with the unique and pure individuality of each human being.

dinal - outward orientation, values derived
from surroundings
adatation to external circumstances

ed - regressive movement of energy, which
demands consciousness adapt to inner norms
- main unconscious concern is to straighten
out their own unconscious contents
- cross of crisis

table - no fixed direction for its energy
- plays dual role progressiv ⇄ regres

Elements = viewing/evaluating/
a provider info about content
Fire - intuition - self centered, the future; possibility
     - discovery, appearance
     - perceives what coffee cup might do

EARTH - sensation; practical - concrete - factual
       - perceives coffee cup concretely

Air - thinking
    - distinguishes coffee cup among phenom

Water - feeling
      - feels whether coffee cup is beautiful
        or pleasant to drink from.

Signs - potential
Houses - circumstances
Personal Contents - ☉ ☽ ☿ A
Elements represent 4 cal view of world
Crosses symbolize way assimilate all processes.

Crosses show how someone adapts to events & circumstances